♻Going GREEN

Hints & Tips to Reduce Your Carbon Footprint

Going GREEN

Hints & Tips to Reduce Your Carbon Footprint

VIVIAN HEAD

Abbeydale Press

ISBN 978-1-86147-268-7

1 3 5 7 9 10 8 6 4 2

Published by Abbeydale Press
an imprint of Bookmart Ltd
Registered number 2372865
Trading as Bookmart Ltd
Blaby Road, Wigston, Leicester
LE18 4SE, England

Produced by Omnipress Limited, UK
Cover design by Omnipress Limited, UK

Printed in Dubai

THE AUTHOR

VIVIAN HEAD lives in East Sussex and is both a designer
and an author. She has written extensively on many
subjects and her books make both an interesting and
factual read. She has co-written another title in this
series entitled *Green Cleaning*.

DISCLAIMER

These ideas are passed on in good faith but the
authors do not guarantee results, nor cannot be held
responsible for any adverse results.

CONTENTS

WHY IS IT SO IMPORTANT?

YOUR CARBON FOOTPRINT

I am certain everyone is aware of the term 'carbon footprint', but do you really know what it means?

A carbon footprint is something that is used to measure the amount of harm caused by an individual, an entire household, an institution or business through their damaging carbon dioxide emissions, or the amount of greenhouse gases that are produced. To try and sustain our rapidly changing environment, it is essential that we all attempt to reduce our carbon dioxide emissions as far as is feasibly possible.

Although this might sound like a daunting task, there are many small ways in which you can play your part. For example, think very carefully before you throw something away and assess whether it can be recycled. Try to reduce the amount of times you fly to your holiday destination. Try using public transport as much as possible, or alternatively take to walking or cycling as an alternative means of getting around. If you have to use your car for work, find out about the possibilities of signing up for a car share scheme. All these, and many more actions which will be mentioned later in the book, will help to reduce your carbon footprint.

Another way of helping the environment is to plant trees to offset the carbon. Because trees breathe in carbon dioxide and convert it into oxygen — a process called sequestration — this is not only an inexpensive but an exceptionally rewarding way of contributing to the well-being of our environment. Next time you sit out in your garden enjoying the sun, just remember that all the plants in your garden are playing their part to make this a better world to live in.

Don't just shrug your shoulders and say, 'What difference can I make?' Do something positive for our planet today — you, and thousands of others like you, WILL make a difference if not immediately, then for the benefit of the next generation. Be aware that the resources on our planet are not finite and will eventually run out. In fact, some of our natural resources have already been depleted and it is down to us to realise that if we don't do something about it now, our only legacy will be a trail of devastation for our children and grandchildren.

In truth, 'Going Green' is no longer an option, it is a necessity. Starting today, make it your own personal mission to do everything possible to stop global warming — after all, it is down to us as human beings to stop the situation getting worse.

THE GREENHOUSE EFFECT

The Industrial Revolution began in England around 1733 with the opening of the first cotton mill. It was a period of major changes in agriculture, manufacturing and transportation, all of which had a radical effect on society as a whole. As more and more industries opened, the demand for energy to run their machines steadily increased. The energy was provided by fossil fuels like coal and oil, but burning these fuels released toxic greenhouse gases. Added to that, many of the workers became sick and died as a result of the toxic fumes, while others were severely injured while working the dangerous machinery. Although the Industrial Revolution did have its good side, it also started dramatic changes in our climate.

The natural greenhouse effect is something that is created by the heat radiated by the Sun and other natural gases that are present in our atmosphere. Without the atmosphere life on Earth could not survive, but the problem is that our atmosphere is changing, and very rapidly. Many of our favourite activities, such as flying and driving, are polluting the atmosphere and producing gases. It is the build-up of these gases that is having such a devastating effect on the planet we call home.

WHAT ARE GREENHOUSE GASES?

Greenhouse gases are emissions that rise into the atmosphere and trap the Sun's energy, keeping heat from escaping. The most important of these gases is carbon dioxide, also known as CO_2. Every time a human or animal breathes out, they release CO_2, but there is absolutely nothing we can do about that.

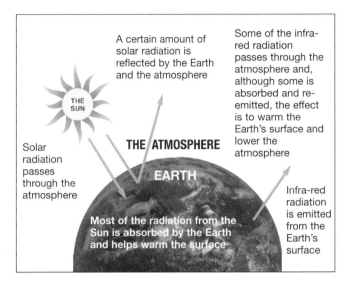

A certain amount of solar radiation is reflected by the Earth and the atmosphere

Some of the infra-red radiation passes through the atmosphere and, although some is absorbed and re-emitted, the effect is to warm the Earth's surface and lower the atmosphere

THE SUN

Solar radiation passes through the atmosphere

THE ATMOSPHERE

EARTH

Infra-red radiation is emitted from the Earth's surface

Most of the radiation from the Sun is absorbed by the Earth and helps warm the surface

However, there is something we can do about the main source of CO_2 in our atmosphere — the burning of fossil fuels such as coal, oil, petrol and wood.

Nitrogen oxide is another type of greenhouse gas. This gas is discharged into the atmosphere every time we drive a car and also by coal-burning power plants as they generate our electricity which we use so liberally.

The third major greenhouse gas is methane. This is created by rotting plants but, more importantly, by all our rubbish as it decomposes in landfill sites. As a side note it is worth mentioning, just for interest, that every time an animal or human suffers from flatulence they are actually releasing methane into the air!

Many chemical compounds found in the Earth's atmosphere act as natural greenhouse gases. It is these gases that allow sunlight to enter the atmosphere of its own accord. When sunlight hits the Earth's surface, some of it is reflected back towards space as infra-red radiation (or heat). (*See the diagram on page 11.*) Greenhouse gases absorb this infrared radiation, which has the effect of trapping the heat in the atmosphere just above Earth's surface. Over time, the amount of energy sent back to Earth from the Sun, should be approximately the same amount of energy radiated back into space. As long as this continues to happen, the temperature on Earth's surface will remain roughly constant.

However, if the atmosphere accumulated all the trapped heat, then the Earth's temperature would continue to rise until it was totally out of control. As long as the balance of greenhouse gases remains the same, and as long as the heat we receive from the Sun remains constant, then an equilibrium is established. In equilibrium, the natural greenhouse effect maintains the average temperature of Earth at 16°C (60.8°F).

CHANGES IN OUR ATMOSPHERE

Earth's atmosphere is made up of 78 per cent nitrogen, 21 per cent oxygen, with just 1 per cent of natural greenhouse gases. Although this might seem rather a small proportion, this comparatively minimal amount of natural greenhouse gases makes an enormous difference.

Before the Industrial Revolution the mixture of gases that made up the atmosphere remained relatively constant. However, with the Revolution came a rapid increase in the world's population. This increase meant that more of the gases that cause the greenhouse effect were released into the atmosphere.

This is not just conjecture. Over the last few years scientists have been able to analyse air bubbles trapped in ancient ice, giving them accurate measurements. There is now clear evidence that levels of carbon dioxide, methane, nitrous oxide and halocarbons are increasing all the time. Many of these scientists believe that these increasing concentrations of greenhouse gases will lead to an increase in the world's average temperature. This is what they call the 'enhanced greenhouse effect'.

As global temperatures rise, this would bring changes to whole planet and affect every nation. This makes the greenhouse effect an international matter, and every country needs to play their part before the pollution to our atmosphere escalates out of control.

Carbon dioxide
Carbon dioxide is a colourless, odourless and non-flammable gas which is recycled through the atmosphere by the process called photosynthesis. This cycle is essential for us to exist on Earth. Photosynthesis is the process of plants and other organisms converting light energy into chemical energy.

Carbon dioxide is also discharged into the air as we exhale, when we burn fossil fuels and by deforestation. It is estimated that every year humans add over 30 billion tons of carbon dioxide to the atmosphere by these activities alone. Deforestation is one of the main producers of carbon dioxide, when large areas of forest are cleared for wood, pulp and fuel. Forests and wooded areas are essential for absorbing the excess of carbon dioxide, and deforestation on such a large scale means that photosynthesis cannot take place. As the number of trees declines, less carbon dioxide is being recycled.

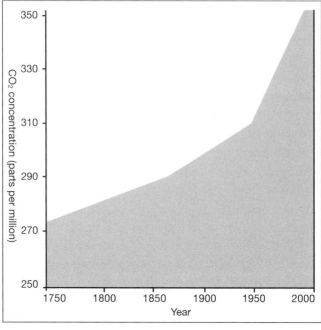

Graph showing increase of carbon dioxide in the atmosphere since 1750.

As we burn large areas of forest, huge amounts of carbon dioxide are released into the atmosphere, adding greatly to the greenhouse effect. It is estimated that an area the size of Central Park in New York – about 860 acres (3.5 sq km) – is being destroyed every 15 minutes. So as you can see, this contributes greatly to the overall greenhouse effect.

Methane
Methane is a colourless, odourless and flammable gas which is formed when plants decompose. It is sometimes known as 'swamp gas' because of its abundance in wet and swampy areas. Bacteria that can be found in cows, sheep, goats, buffalo, termites and camels produce methane naturally and assist in breaking down organic matter in wetlands.

Although there is a very low proportion of methane in the atmosphere, since 1750 the quantity of this gas has doubled and it is believed it could double again by the year 2050. Every year we are building up the amount of methane in the air by raising livestock, coal mining, drilling for oil and natural gas, the cultivation of rice and allowing our rubbish to decay in landfill sites. Owners of the rice paddies are already doing their part by trying new harvesting techniques, which can significantly reduce methane emissions and increase yields.

Livestock and termites are large producers of methane. Bacteria in the gut of the animal break down food and convert a portion of it into methane. When a cow belches, methane is released, and in one

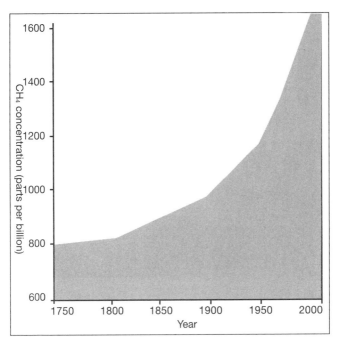

Graph showing increase of methane in the atmosphere since 1750.

day a cow can emit as much as half a pound of methane. Multiply this by as many as 1 billion and you can see the effect it can have!

Methane only stays in the atmosphere for approximately 10 years and yet it can trap 20 times more heat than carbon dioxide. Molecule for molecule, methane is 20 times more potent than carbon dioxide as a greenhouse gas. It is now believed that methane emissions may account for as much as a third of the total climate warming. The rising methane level is also the main cause of rising ozone levels.

Nitrous oxide
Despite its relatively small concentration in the atmosphere, nitrous oxide is the third largest greenhouse gas that contributes to overall global warming.

Nitrous oxide is a gas that is emitted by bacteria in the soil and our oceans and has been a part of Earth's atmosphere for a long time. Agriculture is the main source of human-produced nitrous oxide, created when we cultivate the soil, when we use nitrogen fertilisers and in the handling of animal and human waste waste. Livestock — primarily cows, chickens and pigs — produce around 65 per cent of human-related nitrous oxide. Industrial sources make up only about 20 per cent and include the production of nylon, nitric acid and the burning of fossil fuels in internal combustion engines.

It is a colourless gas with a sweet odour, which is primarily used as an anaesthetic because it deadens pain — also known as 'laughing gas'. Since 1750 nitrous oxide emissions have risen by more than 15 per cent, and this increase is mainly down to our use of nitrogen-based fertilisers, the disposal of human and animal waste in sewage treatment plants and exhaust fumes from our cars. It is vital that we start to reduce our emissions of this gas because it will be still trapped in our atmosphere in 100 years' time.

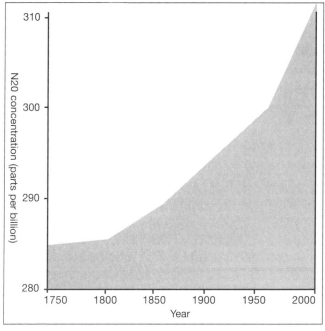

Graph showing increase of nitrous oxide in the atmosphere since 1750.

Chlorinated flurocarbons (CFCs)

Thomas Midgeley discovered in the 1930s that dichlorodifluoromethane could be used as a refrigerant because it could be easily converted from a gas into a liquid. Because of this property it has been used in the production of refrigerators, air conditioners and aerosol cans. The problem with CFCs is that they are very unreactive and therefore stay in the atmosphere for a long time — anything up to 100 years. This gives them plenty of time to be transported to the stratosphere where, with the help of ultraviolet light, they react with the ozone layer. Another problem with CFCs is that they are a thousand times more active than carbon dioxide, so very small concentrations of this gas can have very large effects.

Fortunately since the Montreal Protocol in 1987, there have been many international agreements to restrict the use of CFCs. The substitute for CFCs is hydrofluorocarbons (HFCs) which do not harm or break down the ozone layer. However, they do trap heat in the atmosphere, making it a greenhouse gas which is still having an effect on global warming. The way we can try and reduce the emissions from HFCs is to make sure the coolant is recycled and that we are extra cautious when throwing our old appliances away. Make sure that the coolant is separated from the equipment before it is dumped.

The reason CFCs are so dangerous to the atmosphere is because when they are released and interact with sunlight, they release chlorine atoms. As these atoms rise into the atmosphere they attack and gradually destroy parts of the protective ozone layer.

Although many countries agreed to cut the use of CFCs substantially by the year 2000, in theory the damage has already been done. The existing chemicals in our atmosphere will continue to destroy the ozone layer for at least 100 years.

Ozone
Ozone is an invisible gas — a form of oxygen. A thin layer of ozone exists between 15 to 50 km (9 to 30 miles) above the Earth in the stratosphere, and helps to form a protective shield against the harmful ultraviolet rays emitted by the Sun. However, if ozone

is lower down in the atmosphere it becomes a problem and can cause a photochemical smog. Ozone in itself is an irritant, toxic gas and large concentrations near ground level are dangerous for our health. Perhaps of even greater importance is that this presence of ozone, being a greenhouse gas, is contributing to global warming. 1n 1985, scientists discovered that the ozone layer was not just getting thinner, but that there was actually quite a large hole in it over Antarctica. In fact, the hole was so large that it covered an area the size of the entire USA. Another hole was discovered in 1988, this time over the Arctic, and they found that the holes were constantly changing in shape and size depending on the season.

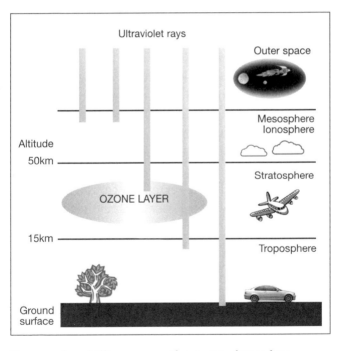

For nearly a billion years, the ozone layer has protected life on Earth from the harmful effects of ultraviolet rays.

EFFECTS OF GLOBAL WARMING

As greenhouse gases increase in Earth's atmosphere, we will experience many environmental problems.

- Increased water vapour in the atmosphere
- Glacier and polar ice caps would melt
- The melting ice would cause sea levels to rise resulting in flooding
- Some places on Earth would become too hot to live in
- Droughts would become more severe and widespread
- Crops and livestock would suffer
- Health problems would be more widespread

Scientists now estimate that the average temperatures on Earth could rise by between 3 and 10°F by the middle of the next century. That rise would have disastrous effects which in turn would have major repercussions. As the temperature rises, many living creatures could die and become extinct, while pests like rats and mosquitoes would thrive in the warmer climate.

As the seas warm up and increase the humidity in the air, this will encourage tropical cyclones and change wave patterns which could produce tidal waves and beach erosion all along our coasts.

Some of the greenhouse gases are absorbed naturally — sea water soaks up carbon dioxide and so do the tiny organisms called plankton. However, the water needs to be cold for the plankton to do its job, so if the seas warm up, even by just a few degrees, the plankton will absorb far less carbon dioxide.

Plants on land also soak up carbon dioxide, especially the trees in the rainforests around the world. However, because so many of these trees are being cut down and burned to make clearings, there are fewer trees to absorb the carbon dioxide. What is even worse, though, is that the burning actually produces carbon dioxide, which, in itself, is contributing to the greenhouse effect. In fact it is this act of deforestation that is one of the major causes of the greenhouse effect.

Modern civilisations have built their lives around a more or less predictable climate over the past centuries. Generations of people have built their homes around the coastlines, believing that the tides would rise and flow more or less to the same level year by year. They have used dams to stem rivers that are affected by snow melt every spring. Dug dykes that can withstand rough seas and even built irrigation systems to carry water to areas that rarely see any rainfall. Farmers plant their crops according to the seasonal rainfall and to avoid the worst frosts, however these things that have been taken for granted in the past could all change.

Over the next century, Earth will see progressively rising temperatures and we are already seeing the effects. There is evidence of changing sea levels, retreating glaciers and many more incidents of extreme weather. The overwhelming majority of scientists believe it is not a matter of IF the climate will change, but WHEN and by HOW MUCH.

Global warming could also lead to many more health concerns. Insects and pests will thrive, thus carrying diseases such as malaria and dengue fever further afield. Cholera would probably be widespread due to the algae becoming toxic in the warmer sea water. The most obvious threat, however, is from the heat itself. With an undoubted increase in heatwaves, there will be many more people suffering from heatstroke and exhaustion, heart attacks and other ailments that are aggravated by the heat. For example, in July 1995 — the hottest year since records began — a heatwave killed more than 700 people in the Chicago area alone.

People will also be subjected to problems resulting from dirtier air and water, threats to food supplies and the possible collapse of many ecosystems. As the sea waters rise, they would envelop many of the lands inhabited by people, causing thousands if not millions being forced to leave their homes.

As the air becomes more polluted by all the toxins we are sending up into our atmosphere, so does the rain. At one time you could depend on a good rainfall to help clear the air of pollutants, but now in certain parts of the world even the rain is polluted. This is called 'acid rain'. But what turns harmless rain into a potentially dangerous liquid? Once again it is our burning of fossil fuels, including petrol in our cars and the oil we use for cooking and running our heating systems. The biggest source by far is the burning of coal — especially certain kinds of coal that carry a large amount of sulphur — which is used to fuel our electricity generating plants.

All of these sources release nitrogen oxides or sulphur dioxide into the atmosphere. Once airborne, these two substances combine with other chemicals and water to form sulphuric acid. When these chemicals mix with moisture they fall back to Earth and cause a lot of damage. It poisons fish and other creatures that live in our lakes, rivers and streams. It can kill trees and it has been known to damage some of our most valuable and treasured buildings. Acid rain also affects humans, causing not just lung damage but other major health problems as well. Young children and elderly people who suffer from asthma and other breathing disorders are particularly susceptible.

To summarise, human-induced climate change is already starting to have a major effect on our planet. It is no longer something that we can ignore, saying that it will not affect us in our lifetime — it will and it does. We need to know what we can do to slow down the whole process; so think very carefully before you go about your normal everyday activities.

- Turning on a light
- Watching television
- Listening to your stereo
- Washing or tumble drying clothes
- Using a hair dryer
- Riding in a car
- Using a microwave
- Using air conditioners
- Playing a video game
- Using your dishwasher
- Leaving electrical equipment such as TVs on standby

When you do any of the above things, and many more besides, did you know that you are sending greenhouse gases into the atmosphere? If you think about how many times a day you do these things and multiply that by the number of other people doing the same things — it's a lot of pollution! Now read on and learn what we can do to make a difference.

ALTERNATIVE ENERGY

WHAT ARE BIOFUELS?

Biofuels are any type of fuel made from natural resources or from the waste products they produce, for example:

- wood, wood chippings or straw
- pellets or liquids made out of wood
- biogas (methane) made out of animals' faeces
- ethanol, diesel or other liquid fuels that have been made from processing plant material or waste oil

Biofuel can be broken down into two different categories — ethanol and diesel. Bioethanol, which is an alcohol, is normally mixed with petrol, while biodiesel is either used on its own or in a mixture.

Biodiesel is an alternative fuel to regular diesel and can be produced from straight vegetable oil, animal oil/fats, tallow and waste cooking oil. The process used to convert these oils to biodiesel is called transesterification — the reaction of the oil to an alcohol. Transesterification of vegetable oils has been used since the mid-1800s and was most probably used to distil glycerine when making soap. The by-products of this process are methyl and ethyl esters, both of which are used in the production of biodiesel.

The largest source for biodiesel comes from oil crops such as rapeseed, palm or soybean. At present the majority of biodiesel produced in the UK is made from waste vegetable oil sourced from restaurants such as fish and chip shops, where they have a lot of waste oil to dispose of. Because this is a cheap way of sourcing the oil (very often it is provided free), biodiesel made in this way can compete with fossil diesel.

Ethanol is produced by fermenting plant sugars such as sugar cane and corn. After fermentation you are left with a watery solution and the ethanol is separated from the water by distillation. Under current specifications, ethanol can only be blended with standard fuel up to 10 per cent in the USA and 5 per cent in Europe. However, neat ethanol or higher concentrations can be used in vehicles that have been specially adapted to run on biofuel.

Biodiesel is produced by a chemical reaction that takes place between vegetable oil — for example rapeseed or soybean oil — and an alcohol. The property of the finished biofuel is very close to diesel fuel and the two can be mixed very easily, resulting in biodiesel. Like ethanol, biodiesel can be used in current vehicles as a blend, or pure in modified cars.

ADVANTAGES OF BIOFUELS

Biofuel has many environmentally beneficial properties, but the main benefit is that it can be described as 'carbon neutral'. In layman's terms this means that the fuel produces no net output of carbon in the form of carbon dioxide. Biofuel produced from plants cannot only help reduce the world's dependence on oil, but also the production of harmful CO_2 emissions. Although the burning of these fuels still releases carbon dioxide, the plants from which they are made absorb a comparable amount of the gas from the atmosphere, making them a much more eco-friendly option.

Biodiesel is rapidly degradable and completely non-toxic, meaning that spillages represent far less of a risk than regular fossil diesel. Also it has a higher flashpoint and is therefore safer in the event of an accident.

Biofuels are already being used globally, with Brazil leading the world in both production and use.
It makes around 16 billion litres of ethanol per year from its sugar cane industry. The most common use for biofuels is automotive transport, and the industry is continually expanding.

The argument against biofuels, from an environmental point of view, is the issue of biodiversity. It is feared that many countries will be even more tempted to replace rainforests with plantations of palm oil, causing further devastation than already is taking place, not only to the climate but to the wildlife as well. The hope for the future is the 'second generation' of biofuels.

Many second generation biofuels are under development, using waste biomass from agriculture and forestry. This form of biofuel could significantly reduce our production of carbon dioxide and will not compete with the production of the world's food crops. Second generation biofuels certainly offer the potential to be the most cost-effective and clean route to low-carbon energy for road transport, but they will not be available in any significant quantities for the next few years.

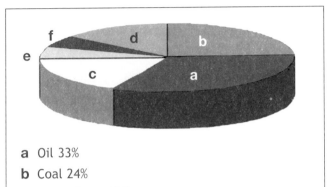

a Oil 33%
b Coal 24%
c Natural gas 18%
d Biomass 14%
e Hydro 6%
f Nuclear 5%

Present percentage of the world's energy production.

HISTORY OF FUEL

Interestingly, humans have been using forms of biomass fuels for heating and cooking ever since the discovery of fire — that was until the discovery of electricity. For a long time humans had tried to harness the power of electricity, especially that produced by lightning. However, it wasn't until 1750 that Benjamin Franklin actually proved that it was electricity by performing his famous experiment with a silk kite and a metal key.

The experiment
Most people have probably heard about Benjamin Franklin's experiment, but perhaps never really understood how it worked. In an effort to harness the power from lightning, Franklin flew a kite during a thunderstorm with a Leyden jar — an early device for

storing electric charge — attached to the silk string of the kite. As a storm cloud passed overhead, a negative charge leaked onto his kite, the string and the Leyden jar which was attached by a thin metal wire. However, Franklin was not affected by the negative charges because he was holding a dry silk string which had the effect of insulating him from the charges going through the jar. However, when Franklin reached out to touch the jar he received an electric shock. This was because the negative charges were so strongly attracted to the positive charges in Franklin's body, that a spark jumped from the jar to his hand. This went to prove that lightning was actually static electricity.

In 1771, 21 years later, Luigi Galvani made an interesting discovery when he found that a dead frog would twitch when it was touched by two pieces of metal, copper and iron. He found that it caused an electrical current to travel through the frog's body, causing it to move — something they called galvanism. Galvani's associate, Alessandro Volta, using the information his friend had given him, managed to develop the voltaic pile, which was a forerunner to the modern-day battery. Finally, Sir Humphrey David devised a way of connecting voltaic piles and invented the first battery as we know it.

Today, humans rely helplessly on a regular supply of electricity to run their homes and businesses. Electricity has been generated for this purpose since 1881, with the first power plants being run on water or coal. Present day plants rely mainly on coal, nuclear, natural gas, hydroelectric and petroleum, with a very small proportion using eco-friendly supplies of solar energy, tidal harnesses, wind turbines and geothermal sources. Hopefully with time, the use of these supplies will increase as concerns over greenhouse gas emissions become more widespread. It is hoped that the increased use of biomass energy will help to reduce our dependence on fossil fuels.

HISTORY OF THE DIESEL ENGINE

Rudolph Diesel developed the theory for the diesel engine in 1892 and published a paper the following year entitled *The Theory and Construction of a Rational Heat Engine*. This paper described a revolutionary system in which air was compressed by a piston to an exceptionally high pressure, having the effect of creating a high temperature. Fuel was then injected and ignited by the compression temperature, driving the piston down. Diesel was a well-respected thermal engineer and social theorist and, within a few years, his design became the standard of the world. He filed for a patent for his new invention in 1894, which then became known as the diesel engine, the first of its kind to prove that fuel could successfully be ignited without using a spark.

Diesel's vision was that his innovative engine would give independent craftsmen, artisans and those he classed as the 'common people', the chance to compete with the larger industries which were powered by the oversized, expensive and fuel-wasting steam engine. He spent the next two years improving his engine and by the end of 1896 was able to demonstrate the first diesel engine which would be suitable for practical use. This engine operated at an amazing effeciency of 75 per cent.

By 1898 Diesel was a millionaire and his engines were used to power pipelines, electric and water plants, cars and lorries and certain marine craft. From there the uses were endless — mines, oil fields, factories and transoceanic shipping — and big industry was now taking advantage of his invention.

However, that was not the end of Diesel's vision. His dream was that diesel engines should be run on biofuels, including vegetables, seed oils and even hemp. At the 1990 World Fair, Diesel proved that his engine could run on peanut oil — the original biodiesel. As a result of Diesel's vision, compression ignited engines were powered by a biomass fuel — vegetable oil — at least until the 1920s.

Ralph Diesel mysteriously disappeared in 1913 and there is much controversy over the timing of his death. Although at the time it was thought that he may have committed suicide or that it had just been a tragic accident, others suggested that it possibly had a political motivation. At the time of his death Diesel had shown his dissent regarding the politics of Germany and was not keen on their naval fleet using his engine to power their ships. His allegiance was towards France and England, despite his Bavarian background, and he was on his way to England to arrange for them to use his engine when he inexplicably disappeared over the side of the ship in the English Channel. This meant that there was now nothing to stop the Germans using the diesel engine to power their submarines.

The first diesel engine that was small enough to power cars was the Type 260D, introduced by Mercedes-Benz in 1936. However, the 1920s were a time of great change and the diesel engine was fast becoming a major challenge for the biofuel industry. The petroleum companies were expanding and starting to establish themselves within the fuel industry, and diesel engines were altered to utilise the lower viscosity of the fossil fuel rather than biodiesel.

The wealth of many of the oil tycoons, and their already influential presence in the industry, exacerbated the obscurity of biofuel production, making sure that the public were not aware that there was an alternative way to fuel their cars.

Like Rudolph Diesel, Henry Ford shared the vision that plant-based fuels were the way forward and, in partnership with Standard Oil, he helped further the biofuel industry. He encouraged the development of production plants and distribution stations but, as with biodiesel, his vision was quashed by the petrol companies and ethanol vanished without a trace.

Hopefully the 21st century will see far more advancement and our dependency on fossil fuels will drive us to explore more and more alternatives.

RUNNING YOUR
CAR ON VEGETABLE OIL

Firstly, it is essential to point out that regular petrol cars are not suitable to run on biodiesel. Your car MUST have a diesel engine and not all diesel engines are suitable; you would need to check with your manufacturer before changing over. Also, to run your car totally on vegetable oil you would still have to make some modifications to your vehicle even if it has a diesel engine. Vegetable oil in its natural state is too viscous to use directly, because the glycerine content could cause coking of the fuel injector heads and damage to the injector pump which might lead to engine failure. However, there are two ways of reducing this viscosity:

First, by removing the glycerine to make biodiesel, in which case no conversion is necessary.

Second, by converting your vehicle to use neat vegetable oil. Using this method, the modifications would heat the oil which reduces the viscosity.

If you do not wish to go to the expense and time of converting your vehicle, it is possible to mix biodiesel with regular diesel, but it would be advisable to seek advice on the preferred ratio. Running your car on vegetable oil as a biofuel makes it virtually carbon neutral. This means that the carbon dioxide released when the oil is burnt is absorbed by the plants that will provide the next crop of oil.

The emissions your car produces will also be cleaner — sulphur is eliminated and a whole range of other pollutants are dramatically reduced. Other benefits include the fact that it is non-toxic, biodegradable, and your original source will never run out.

If you feel it is worth the effort, your car will become far more environmentally friendly and there are plenty of books and kits to help you if you wish to tackle the task yourself. All kits now come with upgraded, more informative instructions to help you make the final transition.

Running your car on vegetable oil can also save you money because since the law changed in July 2007, it is now legal to make up to 2,500 litres of your own biodiesel, which is enough to run the average family car but without paying any tax.

In many European countries, a 5 per cent biodiesel blend is already being used and is available at thousands of petrol stations, particularly in France which is one of the largest biofuel consumers. The diesel is coded with a 'B' prefix followed by a number, i.e. 5, which indicates the percentage of biodiesel added. It is hoped that the UK will very soon follow the example of its European neighbours.

Converting your car

This section is by no means an instruction manual. I aim to give just a few useful hints and tips to get you started. First of all you will need to find out whether your car is suitable for conversion. If you are in any doubt at all about putting biofuels into your car, contact the manufacturer of your vehicle who will be able to advise you.

Another word of warning is to anyone with a brand new car that is still under warranty. You would need to make absolutely sure that it is approved by your dealer otherwise you may make your warranty null and void.

Then you need to decide where you would like to source your vegetable oil. You can buy oil from supermarkets, or for a cheaper alternative you can approach your local fish and chip shop or other restaurant or pub that has to dispose of its waste cooking oil. Although not everyone will relish the thought of refining old chip fat, it can be interesting and fun, and of course you have to remember that you are reducing your impact on the environment.

Once you get the oil home — if you are using recycled vegetable oil — you will need to make certain refinements. For full details on how to refine your oil into biodiesel, there is plenty of information on websites, forums and in books — so get reading.

It is worth mentioning that no special tools are required to do the conversion and it is not beyond the capabilities of the average DIY enthusiast. The main aim is to heat the vegetable oil so that it is not too viscous to cloy your engine.

Two-tank method
For this method you will need to install an extra tank to hold the diesel. Your car is started from the diesel tank and then when the engine is hot you can switch over to the main tank containing the oil, which is heated continually using a heat exchange system. Using this method you will need to swap back to your diesel tank before stopping, to ensure that there is enough diesel in your engine and fuel line when you come to start your car again.

One-tank method

This is possibly the simpler method because you don't have to remember to switch back to regular diesel at the end of each journey. In this method you can mix vegetable oil and diesel in the same tank. This one-tank conversion involves preheating the vegetable oil before it reaches the cylinders. It is essential to install a new, wider fuel line between the fuel tank and the heat exchanger, and the engine is often optimised to run on vegetable oil with modified injectors — this is due to the extra viscosity of the vegetable oil.

Making your own biodiesel

Of course, if you don't want to convert your engine, then you do have the option of making your own biodiesel. There are many courses being run to give you guidance and once mastered it is not too daunting a task. Added to that, it will be far better and cheaper than the diesel sold to you by the big oil companies. Also your engine will run better and last longer, and of course it is much cleaner, better for the environment and your own health. If you make it from recycled oil it will not only be relatively cheap but you are helping to get rid of a troublesome waste product as well.

If you would like to take the challenge to make your own biodiesel there are three basic steps:

- base catalysed transesterification of the vegetable oil;
- direct avid catalysed transesterification of the oil;
- conversion of the oil to its fatty acids and then to biodiesel.

Almost all biodiesel is produced by using the transesterification method, as it is by far the most economical and will produce a 98 per cent conversion yield. The transesterification process is the reaction of vegetable oil with an alcohol to form esters and glycerol.

The following is a brief explanation of the transesterification process, but for full details of how to make your biodiesel it will be necessary to follow precise instructions from a book or website.

The normal catalyst used for this process is sodium hydroxide (caustic soda) or ethanol. Both of these solutions will need to be handled with care as they are dangerous chemicals. The mixture is dissolved in an alcohol using an agitator or mixer. This mixture is then put into a closed reaction vessel and the vegetable oil is added. From this point the vessel needs to remain closed to prevent any evaporation of the alcohol. The mixture in the reactor needs to be kept just above the boiling point of alcohol — approximately 160°F/71°C — to speed up the reaction process. This can vary from one to eight hours.

Once the reaction is complete, you are left with two major products — glycerine and biodiesel. These two products need to be separated and as the glycerine is far more dense it should have settled at the bottom of the vessel and can simply be drawn off.

After the two components have been separated, the excess alcohol needs to be removed. This is done with a flash evaporation process or by distillation.

The recovered alcohol can be kept and reused, although it is essential that no water accumulates in the recovered alcohol.

Once the biodiesel has been separated from the glycerine and the alcohol removed, it is sometimes purified by washing gently with warm water to remove any residual catalyst or soaps. In some processes this step is not necessary, but it depends on the system you are using.

After all these steps you should be left with a colourless, odourless biodiesel which, after checking carefully that it is ready for use, can be put directly into your diesel car.

BIOMASS

There is a wealth of energy to harness by using the abundance of plants and animals that live alongside mankind. Power generated by using organic matter is called biomass energy or bioenergy. One form of bioenergy is the gas called methane, which is a naturally occurring by-product of decaying plant and animal matter commonly found in bogs, wetlands and even landfill sites. The use of biomass fuels could not only significantly contribute to the disposal of waste products but it could also help prevent climate change. As the cost of heating with natural gas and fuel oils continues to rise, people are being pushed towards the use of biomass fuels as an alternative form of generating heat.

Biomass is carbon based and is composed of a mixture of organic molecules. However, the carbon used to construct biomass is absorbed from the atmosphere by plant life, using energy from the Sun. These processes have happened for as long as there have been plants on Earth and is part of what we call the 'carbon cycle'.

When biomass fuels are burned, the energy is released as heat. If you have a wood burner or open fireplace, the wood you burn is a biomass fuel. The waste from wood or our rubbish can also be burned to produce steam for making electricity. Biomass continues to be a major source of energy in much of the developing world, and many industries producing wood and paper products use their own waste products to produce steam and electricity. This not only saves the company money as they don't have to dispose of their waste, but also they don't have the expense of buying electricity from an outside source.

Biomass is a renewable, low carbon fuel and its production brings both environmental and social benefits. If used correctly, biomass is a sustainable fuel that can significantly help to reduce our net carbon emissions when compared with fossil fuels.

BIOMASS FROM LANDFILL SITES

Using rubbish from landfill sites to create fuels can contribute to successful waste management, reduce greenhouse emissions and reduce pollution. Landfill sites generate gases as the rubbish buried starts to undergo anaerobic digestion. These gases are collectively known as landfill gas. This gas can be burned and is considered to be a reliable source of renewable energy. It can be burned either directly for heat or to generate electricity for public use.

If this landfill gas is not used, methane escapes into the atmosphere, adding to the global warming problem. Over a time span of 100 years, methane gas would potentially be 23 more times dangerous than carbon dioxide emissions. One landfill power plant could power up to 2,000 homes and would eliminate 6,000 tons of methane every year from getting into the atmosphere.

Remember, change can only really come about from the action of individuals. Industry uses a huge amount of energy, as do households, which account for 30 per cent of the energy used in the UK. Through a combination of reducing the amount of energy we use, by using energy efficiently and by changing to renewable forms of energy, we will be able to protect our environment for future generations.

THE BENEFITS OF USING BIOMASS AS A FUEL

- Biomass can easily be sourced locally from within the UK without any fear of shortage of supply.
- Biomass gives companies the chance to support the rural economy.
- By establishing local networks for production and usage of biomass fuels, it allows both financial and environmental costs of transport to be minimised.
- Many biomass fuels generate lower levels of such atmospheric pollutants as sulphur dioxide, which is one of the contributary factors to acid rain.
- The majority of modern biomass combustion systems are now highly sophisticated and compare favourably with the best fossil fuel boilers.
- Biomass fuels can help with the major problem of pollution from our landfill sites.
- The production of biomass fuels is one way of creating rural infrastructure and, perhaps just as important, it can create lots of jobs.

OTHER FORMS OF RENEWABLE ENERGY

At present the world relies heavily on fossil fuels like coal, oil and natural gas for its energy. Unfortunately these fuels are non-renewable and will eventually run out. Not only do these fuels draw on the Earth's finite resources and damage the environment, but they are becoming increasingly expensive as well. The use of fossil fuels is now accepted worldwide as contributing to global warming, and so hopefully with advanced technology, we can turn to renewable energy to provide our everyday needs.

Renewable energy describes energy produced from natural resources such as sunlight, wind, rain, tides and geothermal heat, all of which replenish

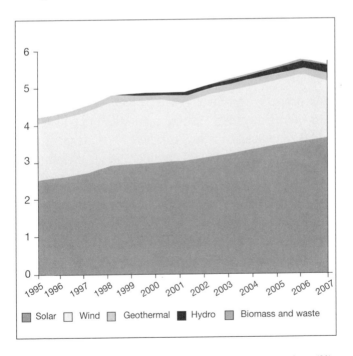

Approximate shares in total energy consumption (%).

themselves naturally. At the present time, however, only around 13 per cent of the world's primary energy comes from renewable energy. Our windswept island has an enormous amount of wind, wave and tidal power, all of which could be harnessed to provide more than enough energy for all our needs. Worldwide there has been a rapid rise in the development and deployment of renewable energy sources, mainly because their use normally entails no (or very little) greenhouse gas emissions and therefore does not contribute to global climate change.

Home Information Packs (HIPS)

It is worth mentioning while we are on the topic of renewable energy, that HIPS are now required for properties on the market with three bedrooms or more in England and Wales. The rating works on how energy efficient your property is and a low rating will decrease the value. So rather than have to spend a lot of time and investment in making your property as 'green' as possible, why not start today.

Your property will be assessed by an Energy Assessor, and will be awarded a rating somewhere between A and G, and nowadays it is estimated that as many as 70 per cent of buyers will consider energy efficiency as an important selling point. Check below to see how you can give your house a higher rating.

A rated houses have:
Solar thermal panels
Wind turbines
Low energy light bulbs
Loft insulation
Thermostat controls
Triple glazing windows
Efficient boiler

G rated houses have:
Wooden floors
Draughty windows
No loft insulation
Cavity walls
Oil boiler
Low energy 'white goods'
Old thermostats

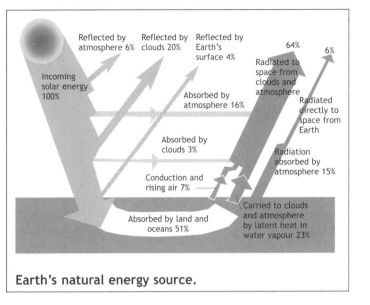

Earth's natural energy source.

SOLAR ENERGY

Even without harnessing it, solar energy plays an enormous part in contributing to our energy by keeping the Earth's surface warm. In fact without its radiant energy, Earth would not support human life. Despite our knowledge of the Sun's power, its use as an energy source is relatively untapped.

The Sun itself has a surface temperature of 6000°C (10,832°F) which is maintained by continuous nuclear fusion reactions between hydrogen atoms which are deep within the planet's interior. Eventually these atoms will convert all of the hydrogen into heavier elements, but this is an exceedingly slow process and the Sun will continue to provide us with its power for at least another five billion years.

The Earth is 150 million kilometres away from the Sun, and yet it can still absorb huge amounts of energy, even though approximately one-third is reflected away by the atmosphere before it reaches us. Just imagine a continuous, inexhaustible supply of power that amounts to 10,000 times our current rate of consumption of fossil fuels, that is always on tap. On a bright, sunny day, the Sun shines approximately 1,000 watts of energy per square metre of the planet's surface and if we were able to collect all of this energy we would be able to power our houses and businesses for free.

When a building is designed specifically to take full advantage of the Sun's heat, the need for additional heating and lighting is minimal. The Sun's rays can also be harnessed by using solar panels to heat water in the same way.

Many Mediterranean countries already use solar power to their advantage and even in Britain, which is covered by cloud for much of the time, there are an estimated 40,000 roof-top solar heating panels. In areas like southern California, which has solar radiation levels more than twice those of the UK, the Sun is strong enough to generate high-temperature steam to power enormous turbines. In fact the world's largest solar thermal-electric installation is the Luz project in California's Mojave Desert.

Solar power can work exceptionally well for most items, with the exception of large electrical appliances that use an electric heat element, for example water heaters, tumble dryers, electric cookers or home heating systems that are run totally by electricity. It would not be cost-effective to use solar power for these items.

The first solar cells

The development of solar cell technology began with the French physicist Antoine-César Becquerel in 1839. During an experiment he observed a photovoltaic effect while he was working with a solid electrode in an electrolyte solution. He noticed that when light fell on the electrode it produced a level of electricity. Becquerel's research was extended by many other physicists, but it remained a mystery for many years as photovoltaic applications had always been used for measuring light (as in a camera's meter) rather than measuring voltage.

Around 50 years later, an American inventor by the name of Charles Fritts, constructed the first true solar cells using junctions formed by coating the semiconductor selenium with an ultrathin, nearly transparent layer of gold. Fritts's devices were very inefficient, transforming less than 1 per cent of the absorbed light into electrical energy.

In 1941 Russell Ohl, another American, invented the first silicon solar cell, a simple device that converted sunlight into electrical energy. Unlike the earlier selenium cells, the silicon cell converted energy much more efficiently. So efficiently, in fact, that for the first time it was possible to use solar cells to power electrical equipment. As soon as people realised the value of his invention, it was put in service to power a small electronic circuit, which was mounted directly onto a telegraph pole.

The basics of solar power

Using solar power to produce electricity is not the same as using the Sun to produce heat. To produce hot air or fluids solar thermal principles are applied. To harness solar energy to provide electricity, involves the use of a different and more sophisticated principle called photovoltaics (PV). A solar (PV) panel is made of a natural element — silicon — which becomes electrically charged when subjected to sunlight. These panels are mounted on a south-facing roof or facade of a building, to take advantage of the maximum amount of solar radiation during peak hours.

Say, for example, you have an average of six hours of peak sunlight each day, then a standard solar panel can produce around 360 watt hours of power each day. As technologies advance, we are starting to see new and more efficient solar panel designs and hopefully the advantages will soon outweigh the use of fossil fuels. Although it would be fair to say that solar power alone is not enough to provide the complete heating and water requirements for a household, it would certainly allow you to halve your bills and halve the amount of carbon dioxide emissions from your house.

The average cost of a DIY solar installation varies between £1,500 and £2,500, depending on the size and type of installation, but you can expect to recover the cost within a few years. If you would like to tackle the job yourself then there are several types of kits on the market.

The use of solar panels to provide hot water is becoming increasingly popular, and a good panel is able to provide the average household with approximately one-third of its annual requirements.

Before embarking on a project of this size it would be advisable to consult an expert in this field to advise you on the most beneficial appliance for your building.

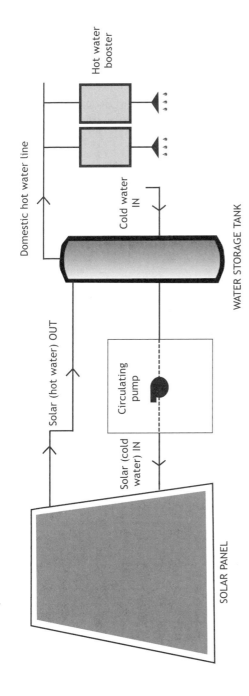

Solar hot water system

Basic solar panel design

A solar panel is made up of a number of smaller cells, each with a voltage of about 0.5 volts. These cells are then mounted onto a heavy and rigid panel of either glass or, for a lighter version, laminated plastic. When these cells are placed in sunlight they start to heat up to about 35–40°C (95–104°F) higher than their surrounding air temperature.

The amount of current that a solar panel can produce is dependent on:

• the amount of sunlight hitting the surface
• the angle of the panel relative to the Sun
• the size of the solar panel

Although the Sun can produce about 1,000 watts of energy per square metre, the solar panel can only convert a fraction of this power into electricity. For optimum performance it is advisable to mount the panel facing south, and it should be tilted to an angle equal to the latitude where it is being used. To get a maximum output, ideally the Sun's rays should strike the solar panel as near to perpendicular as possible.

Although the initial outlay to put solar panels on your home may leave you a little out of pocket, remember that you will soon recoup this money and, more importantly, it will not emit any greenhouse gases.

WIND TURBINES

As mentioned previously, because we live on such a windy island, it makes sense to harness this power to provide us with electricity. Wind power is a large-scale and reliable source of energy, which is already having a very positive impact but, at present, the UK is only using 0.5 per cent wind power to generate electricity. Denmark is currently the world leader in wind power and it is estimated that by 2030, 50 per cent of Denmark's energy could come from the power of the wind.

Modern wind turbines make use of the wind's power to turn aerodynamic blades that turn a rotor which in turn produces electricity. Individual turbines vary a great deal in size and power output, from a few hundred watts to 2–3 megawatts. To give you an idea of the amount of electricity generated, a typical domestic household would require approximately 3–6 kilowatts for its everyday needs. Smaller turbines can be used to power batteries for boats or mobile homes, while larger turbines grouped on wind farms supply electricity to the national grid.

The first wind turbine

Although wind machines were used as early as 200 BC for grinding grain, the first automatically operated wind turbine built to produce electricity was the baby of Charles F. Brush in 1888. At that time it was the largest turbine in the world with a rotor diameter of 17 metres (50 feet) and had 144 separate rotor blades made out of cedar wood. This turbine ran for a period of 20 years and was used to charge the batteries in the cellar of his house.

Despite the size of the first turbine, it only generated a small amount of electricity — 12 kW — and this was due to the fact that the blades rotated fairly slowly and did not work very efficiently. The first fast-rotating wind turbine with fewer rotor blades was discovered by Dane Poul la Cour, and gave a far more efficient level of electricity production.

By the 1930s windmills were quite a common sight on farms in America to generate electricity, and in the UK today, wind power provides enough power to supply 1.2 million homes — and yet this is only just scratching the surface of its full potential.

Large wind farms like the one planned at London Array in the Thames Estuary are currently being planned to provide enough electricity to power 750,000 homes. Some more recently conceived projects are on an even bigger scale, so the long-term potential for wind power is enormous.

Small scale for your home

Because wind speed increases the higher you go, it is best to place your own turbine high up on a mast or tower. Ideally, of course, it should be on top of a hill, clear of any obstructions, but this is not usually a practical option for the average house or building. The rotor blades (usually three) are designed to catch the maximum amount of wind available, and use aerodynamic forces (or lift and drag) in a similar fashion to an aeroplane wing. The blades and shaft are connected to the nacelle, which contains the gearbox and other mechanical components which sit at the top of the turbine tower. This allows the nacelle to rotate freely, and the blades to align with the direction of the wind.

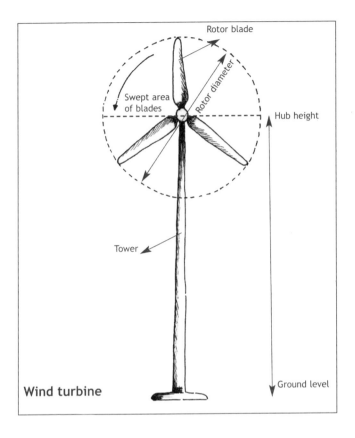

Wind turbine

Small-scale building-integrated wind turbines which are suitable for urban locations have been designed to make the maximum use of wind speed. The wind-speed itself is dependent on a number of factors:
• your location
• height of the turbine from the ground
• number of obstructions
• size of wind turbine and rotors

Like most of the projects in this section, it is as well to seek the advice of a professional before you go to the expense of installing a turbine. If you really are serious about trying to generate your own power by using wind power you will need to take into consideration:

- your local average wind-speed — minimum 6 metres per second or more. An approximate figure for your location can be checked on the BERR website;
- that there are no major obstructions like buildings, trees or hills that are likely to reduce the wind-speed or increase turbulence;
- planning issues also have to be considered, i.e. visual impact, noise and conservation, as you will require local authority permission.

Wind turbines with a 1 kilowatt capacity are designed for domestic buildings and will probably cost you in the region of £1,500. Larger turbines of 2.5 kW up to 6 kW — if you have the space — would cost between £10,000 and £25,000 to install. These costs are inclusive of the turbine, mast, inverters, battery storage (if that is required) and installation. Needless to say, this is only a rough estimate of the cost and the price may vary depending on your location and the type of system you choose.

Turbines generally have a lifespan of around 20 years, but they will require regular service checks to make sure they are working efficiently. If you decide on a battery storage system, then the battery life is around six to ten years and will have to be replaced at some time during the turbine's life.

Although the initial outlay is high, like solar panels you will soon reap the rewards as they will start paying for themselves within a matter of years. One important item to bear in mind, though, is that if there is no wind there is no electricity! Of course, on the plus side, wind power is renewable and produces no greenhouse gases during operation.

POWER OF THE WATER

Unlike solar and wind power, the tide could be a totally reliable source of power as it moves a huge amount of water twice a day with predictability. Although this form of energy is reliable and plentiful, to convert it into a useful form of power, i.e. electricity, is fairly complex. If harnessed, it is believed that almost 10 per cent of the United Kingdom's electricity needs could be met in this way.

But why do we get tides? It has to do with the gravitational force of the Moon and the Sun and the rotation of the Earth. The gravitational attraction of the Moon makes the seas bulge outwards in the direction of the Moon. On the opposite side, another bulge forms as the Earth is being pulled towards the Moon and away from the water on the far side. As the Earth is constantly rotating while this is happening, it causes two major surges (or tides) each day. The first person to really explain tides in any detail was Isaac Newton who was famous for his study of gravity.

To achieve tidal power or tidal energy it is necessary to capture the natural energy created as the water moves in ocean currents and tides. There are two main types of tidal power, the first of which is called kinetic energy, or the energy of motion. The second is potential energy, which comes from the difference between low and high tides, commonly referred to as 'head'.

Kinetic tidal power uses turbines to produce renewable energy. To try and understand this process you need to imagine a giant windmill, but underwater. This form of tidal energy is becoming increasingly popular because its impact on our ecology is far less dramatic than the building of dams, usually referred to as tidal barrages.

Tidal barrages work rather like a hydro-electric system, except that the dam is much larger. The dam is usually built across a river estuary where the tide goes in and out. For this to work the tidal range has to be in excess of 5 metres and its purpose is to let water flow through it into the basin as the tide comes in. At certain points along the dam, turbines are installed and gates which allow the water to pass through. These gates are closed when the tide has stopped coming in, trapping the water within the estuary and creating a hydrostatic head. As the tide starts to recede, the gates in the barrage that contain turbines are opened. The hydrostatic head forces the water through the gates which then drives the turbines to generate electricity.

A prime example of a tidal barrage is at La Rance River in France, where the tidal range is up to 13.4 metres. It has been operating since 1966 and the dam's total width is 760 metres (nearly 0.5 miles). When the tide is high, the dam traps water from the Atlantic and at low tide it allows it to flow back into the sea. En route it passes through 24 turbines which are connected to generators that produce 240 megawatts of power. This provides enough electricity for 300,000 homes and businesses.

Understandably, the higher the tides the more electricity can be generated from a given site and it is estimated that approximately 3,000 gigawatts of energy are currently being produced worldwide from tidal power.

Like solar and wind energy, tidal power is a popular source of renewable energy, mainly because the supply is inexhaustible and, once built, it is relatively cheap to maintain. It produces no greenhouse gases and no other waste, it needs no fuel to run on and it also produces electricity on a regular basis due to the predictability of the tides.

Hydropower

Hydropower has been around for many years, especially in Scotland, and generates approximately 10 per cent of the overall supply of Scottish electricity. Hydropower uses the kinetic energy of moving water. The water passes through a turbine which, in turn, drives a generator that creates electricity. In the same way as the tidal barrage works, the hydropower dam raises the level of the water to create a hydrostatic head. The water is trapped allowing it to be released when necessary, enabling the water to become stored energy.

The advantage of this type of system is that the initial dam requires large investment but, once running, it will generate electricity with no fuel costs. There are also environmental issues regarding the building of a hydroelectric scheme, mainly because it can disrupt the ecosystem around the dam. Firstly, the flow of the river will affect all the aquatic life which, in turn, affects the quality of the water. However, on the plus side, after flooding, the area can be replanted where necessary, attracting new wildlife and becoming a lure for walkers and tourists. At present hydropower is only supplying around 6 per cent of the world's energy and, as one of the most clean and cheapest ways of producing energy, further developments should certainly not be overlooked.

Wave farms

Proponents of clean energy have long seen the seas as a great hope for providing renewable energy; however, technology in this area has been slow to take off. This is starting to change at last with the deployment of wave farms in Portugal and Scotland. In 2007 Scottish engineers embarked on building large devices called the Pelamis system, which is a set of enormous tubes linked together to form a type of hinged 'snake' that will end up at 140 metres (460 feet) long. As the waves travel down the tunnel, each section will move up and down and from side to side, forcing the fluid through generators to produce electricity. The plan is to place 30 of these devices about 5 kilometres out to sea.

The wave farm is expected to supply enough energy for around 15,000 households, and a similar plan is in place for an even larger farm.

GEOTHERMAL ENERGY

Geothermal energy has been used for thousands of years in some countries for both cooking and heating. The name comes from two Greek words — *geo* meaning Earth and *thermal* meaning heat. The energy comes from deep inside the Earth's crust, where the temperature can be as high as 6,000°C (10,832°F), which is hot enough to melt rock. Even just a few kilometres from the surface, the temperature can reach 250°C (482°F) and it is this enormous heat which has been used to generate geothermal power.

Geothermal energy in the form of hot springs has been used for centuries, but the first attempt to generate electricity did not happen until the 20th century. The production of electricity in this way can be an exceptionally efficient way of obtaining renewable energy, but the key to its success is the location of the power station. In fact there are only a very few locations around the world that are capable of producing efficient levels of geothermal electricity. At the present time less than 1 per cent of the world's electricity supply comes from this source.

To harness the energy, deep holes are first drilled through the Earth's surface until a significant geothermal 'hot spot' is discovered. When the precise location has been found, a pipe is put down the hole which allows for hot steam from within the Earth's core to rise up to the surface.

This steam is then channelled into a turbine which starts to turn under the pressure. This turbine is linked to a generator which also turns and then produces electricity. To repeat the process, cold water is sent down a new pipe to be heated by the Earth's natural power and then sent back up the first pipe to start again.

Ground source heat pumps
There are alternative types of geothermal energy systems available which, instead of providing electricity, focus on supplying heat and warmth which, in turn, can heat your water and warm your house. They work on a different system to the power stations, using ground source heat pumps that are put only a few metres below the ground. Water is pumped through one end of a long piece of pipe and by the time it reaches the other end the water is of a significantly higher temperature than when it started. The great advantage to this type of geothermal pump is that it can be used in many different locations, even regions that are covered by snow for a lot of the year.

The ground source heat pump is advantageous for:

- hot water
- underfloor heating
- air-conditioning systems
- heating swimming pools

It is not only an economical form of power, but it is also clean and environmentally friendly. Compared with a regular electric central heating system, a ground source pump system can save you as much as 66 per cent on your annual energy costs. Added to this, there is no combustion inside the house, it is non-polluting and can go a long way to reducing your gas emissions.

A typical heat pump for a domestic dwelling is about the same size as a large fridge and the initial outlay for this would be around £3,000. Of course, the installation cost will add quite a bit to this figure depending on whether you go for bore holes or trenches. There are grants available for 30 per cent of the installation cost and it is worth checking out whether you are eligible on www.heatking.co.uk.

While pointing out the considerable advantages it is also necessary to mention the disadvantages to such a system. The initial cost of design and installation can be high, but this investment would start paying for itself within three years. Secondly, the area needed to lay the rather lengthy piping system can be quite extensive, and consequently may be unsuitable for small developments. In saying this, however, the advantages outweigh the disadvantages greatly, and it is well worth investigating the possibility of using geothermal energy in your home.

SOME SHOCKING STATISTICS

I am going to end this section with a few statistics which hopefully will shock you enough to make you want to do something about making your life greener.

- Did you know that the amount of wood and paper we throw away each year is enough to heat 50 million homes for over 20 years?
- Did you know that a single car driving 1,000 miles (1,609 km) a month emits 120 tons of carbon dioxide every year?
- Did you know that one polystyrene cup contains as many as 1 billion billion molecules of CFCs.
- Did you know that every minute of every day the world is pumping approximately 16 tons of sewage into our waters?
- Did you know that despite the fact that two-thirds of the surface of the Earth is covered with water, all the fresh water in lakes, rivers and streams represents only one-hundredth of the Earth's total water?
- Did you know that every year approximately 1 million seabirds, 100,000 marine mammals and 50,000 seals are killed as a result of eating or being strangled by plastic discarded by humans?
- Did you know that in the precious rainforests of Madagascar, a plant called the rosy periwinkle is used to make drugs that can cure certain kinds of cancer? If we continue to destroy our rainforests plants like this one, and millions of others, will become extinct.
- Did you know that an estimated 25 billion polystyrene coffee cups and 2.5 million plastic bottles are thrown away every hour?
- Did you know that every year we throw away around 40 billion soft drinks cans and bottles? If these were

placed end to end they would reach to the Moon and back nearly 20 times.

- Did you know that approximately 85 per cent of all household rubbish could be recycled?
- Did you know that if you used recycled paper for just one print run of your favourite Sunday newspaper, it could save around 70,000 trees.
- Did you know that if you recycled just one tenth of your newspapers, you could save an estimated 25 million trees every year?
- Did you know that every years 40 million acres of tropical rainforests are being destroyed either through logging or burning.
- Did you know that only 35,000 pesticides introduced since 1945 have been tested for long-term effects on animals and humans.
- Did you know that if you left one 40 watt light bulb on day and night for a year it would use over 350 KWHs?
- Did you know that a dripping tap can waste up to 6,000 gallons of water a month, or 72,000 gallons a year?
- Did you know that it can take as long as 100 years for a plastic bag to decompose?
- Did you know that the average UK household throws away 3 kilograms of food every week?
- Did you know that the average UK household throws away approximately 14 kilograms of food packaging every week?
- Did you know that if you inappropriately dispose of one quart of motor oil it can contaminate up to 2 million gallons of fresh water?
- Did you know that if everyone in the UK drove with properly inflated tyres that we could save nearly 2 billion gallons of petrol every year?
- Did you know that on average British consumers use 290 plastic bags every year, or four bags every five

days, making a total of at least 17.5 billion bags per year?

- Did you know that as many as 800,000 metric tonnes of clothing and shoes were thrown away in one year in the UK?
- Did you know that every time you flush your toilet it uses 3.5–7 gallons on water depending on the size of your cistern?
- Did you know that one bath can use as much as 25–30 gallons of water?
- Did you know that a games console uses as much energy when left in standby mode as it does when it is switched on?
- Did you know that one-third of the average household's cooking energy is used up by an electric kettle? To save energy make sure you only boil the amount of water necessary.
- Did you know that since 1996 the UK has increased its carbon dioxide emissions by about 4.6 million tonnes per year?

Are you shocked? Start today and you will notice that even the smallest changes can not only save you a lot of money but you will be doing your part to save the planet as well. Our daily lives have a great impact on the environment in so many ways, so use this book to help you discover how you can become greener. Each section will guide you through the most important aspects and also provide you with helpful hints and tips.

GOING
SHOPPING

FOOD AND SHOPPING FACTS

It would be fair to say that we are a nation of people who love to shop. Day by day we are bombarded with advertisements encouraging us to buy the latest product on the market. It is very easy for us to forget that many of these new products, and indeed the ones we already use, have a major impact on the environment.

Fortunately this is an area where we can start making a difference straight away without it having to cost a lot of money. For example, buying more organic produce, looking for fair trade labels, avoiding food that has a lot of unnecessary packaging and taking your own bags to the supermarket instead of ending up with hundreds of plastic bags.

TRY NOT TO WASTE FOOD

Before embarking on your next food shopping trip try making a list and buy only the products that you really need. Always make sure that you have a cloth or plastic bag with you so that you don't need to use new plastic bags every time you go out. It is easy to be tempted by the vast array of produce that is displayed to make us buy, but if you stick to your list it will ensure you use everything and hopefully this will cut down on the amount of waste. Also cutting down on your portions can help to avoid throwing away those last bits of uneaten food that you just didn't have room for. Make the changes gradually and you won't find it too daunting.

If you do need to throw food away, make sure you have a compost area at the bottom of your garden. If space is limited or you only have a small courtyard, you could think about buying a compost bin. This topic will be covered in greater detail in the section on recycling.

Start off by avoiding food that contains a lot of packaging, for example buy loose fruit and vegetables. If you do need to buy a product that is packaged make sure the packaging can be recycled, for example glass. Choose carefully between chemically grown food, air-freighted produce, organic and fair trade. Remember, every green choice you make will make a real difference. As you become more aware of what you eat and drink, your shopping trips will become easier and you will be able to feel proud of yourself that you are playing an important part in stopping any further changes to our planet.

PROCESSED FOODS

Much of the food on sale today is highly processed, meaning that it contains a lot of artificial colouring and excesses of salt, sugar and fat to enhance the flavour of what may well be inferior basic ingredients. Using fresh produce rather than processed foods is far better for your health and you will cut down on the amount of waste packaging as well.

If you squeeze your own oranges rather than buying processed juice in a carton, you are helping to shrink your carbon footprint. You can compost your orange leftovers which, in turn, can put nutrients back in the soil, and this is only just one example.

Try to avoid buying white bread, white rice, white pasta, etc. as the outer husk of the grain has been removed. By doing this many of the nutrients have been removed, for example Vitamin B and protein. So it is wise to try to go for wholegrain products.

Fresh fruit and vegetables, either raw or lightly cooked, contain far more goodness than any process ones and you know exactly what you are eating.

On the plus side though, it is far more economical to buy a loaf of bread from your local baker than to make it at home. Heating your oven takes a lot of energy, so unless you are baking other items at the same time it would be more environmentally friendly to go to the professionals who bake many products at one time.

Today, processed foods are being blamed for the sharp rise in cholesterol levels and chronic obesity, so this gives us another reason to turn to naturally healthy products. Processed foods are not only transported long distances from the point of manufacture, but they also spend a long time in their packaging before being eaten. Not only does this add to our carbon dioxide emissions, but the food has to be treated with preservatives to make it survive the journey from manufacture to our table. Meals cooked at home, where we are in control of what we put in them, make a lot more sense and taste a lot better. If we can get our children used to the taste of fresh produce, as opposed to the unnatural flavours of processed foods, we could go a long way to improving the health of our nation.

BUYING ORGANIC

If produce bears an organic label it means that it has had to comply with a set of strict and legally recognised standards. These standards are a guarantee to the consumer that the food has been naturally produced and is free from any form of chemical pesticide or fertiliser. By buying organic food it means that you are supporting the high environmental standards of countryside management.

All organic food is GM (genetic modification) free. Genetically modified foods were first introduced in the early 1990s and refer to crops that have been created for human consumption using the latest molecular biology technologies. The most common GM foods are derived from plants — soybean, corn, canola and cotton seed oil and wheat. Because corn and soya are widely used in food processing, small amounts of these engineered ingredients show up in the majority of processed foods. Scientists are concerned that these engineered organisms may be harmful to a person's health or the environment. For example, engineered crops could contaminate the food supply with drugs, kill insects that are beneficial to our environment and even jeopardise valuable natural resources. It is also feared that GM fish could substantially alter our native ecosystem, perhaps even driving certain wild fish to extinction. Labelling of GM foods has been a contentious issue for a long time, so if possible do not buy any product that shows that it has received outside interference.

Organic farmers have to guarantee the high standard of welfare for their animals, unlike the wording 'Free

Range' which carries very little guarantee. Organic farming is also about keeping the soil healthy so that it is able to absorb the maximum amount of carbon dioxide. If soil is badly managed and treated with chemical fertilisers, it becomes a major source of nitrous oxide, a greenhouse gas which is far more harmful than carbon dioxide. By choosing organic foods and boycotting GM foods you are helping to combat global warming.

FAIRTRADE

Although it is by no means impossible, it is difficult to live entirely on items produced within the UK. Fairtrade is an organised social movement that tries to make sure the farmers get the best price for their crops in the poorer parts of the world. Unfortunately, unfair trading arrangements imposed by powerful rich countries on impoverished ones, have led to an obscene and ever-widening gap between the rich and poor worldwide. Exports play an important role in the world's economy, but it is unfair to exploit workers, many of whom are forced to work in degrading, unhealthy and dangerous conditions for far too little money.

Fairtrade goes part way to providing a solution and there are currently more than 90 coffee, tea, banana, chocolate, cocoa, juice, sugar and honey products carrying the Fairtrade Mark. Fairtrade aims to build up trading relationships between consumers in prosperous countries and producers in the developing countries, which avoid exploitation of both producers and their environment. By doing this, producers receive a guaranteed price for their goods, they have the security of long-term contracts, guaranteed health and safety conditions, and also receive support towards education and other training facilities. Of course, these are all things that we take for granted.

Although the transportation of goods can be a contributory cause of global warming, there are other ways that some of this produce arrives on our shores. Bananas, for example, which keep well, can be transported to Europe in sailing ships, a truly green form of transport. Dried goods like spices, cocoa, grains, pulses and dried fruit do not need to be transported in fuel-hungry refrigerated lorries or planes, as they do not need to get to their destination in a hurry.

If you want more details about where you can buy Fairtrade food, the UK's independent regulator, The Fairtrade Foundation, can give you some detailed information. Alternatively, you can get information from Consumer Direct at the Office of Fair Trading.

By 2007 over 800,000 farmers and workers and their families benefited from Fairtrade sales in the United Kingdom, an estimated 5,000,000 people. Help to make this figure rise by purchasing more Fairtrade products.

SOYA DILEMMA

Soya beans are the seed of the leguminous soya bean plant and have been part of the Chinese diet for thousands of years. They were introduced to Western countries in the 1960s and have since become a sustainable food source. Soya foods include tofu, tempeh, texture vegetable protein which comes in chunks and minced form, miso, soya sauces, soya oil, margarine and soya dairy alternatives. Soya is not only an excellent source of protein, it is also low in

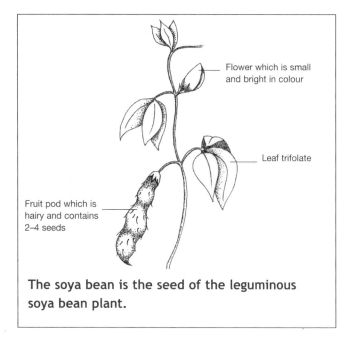

Flower which is small and bright in colour

Leaf trifolate

Fruit pod which is hairy and contains 2–4 seeds

The soya bean is the seed of the leguminous soya bean plant.

saturated fat and cholesterol free, all of which have contributed to high consumption of soya products. However, modern soya bean cultivation is causing major environmental harm. Because of its popularity it has become the subject of intensive farming, leading to the use of chemicals, which, in turn, has caused soil degradation and contamination of ground water.

The demand for soya products has grown rapidly, but unfortunately large areas of pristine rainforest are being destroyed to make way for more production. Land that once supported vital ecosystems could soon be rendered useless due to overfarming and soil degradation. Huge amounts of transportation to move the soya are also adding to the overall damage this one product is causing.

Soya farming has now overtaken cattle ranching and logging as the worst destroyer of the Amazon rainforest. In fact Brazil has been so successful in adapting the soya plant to the tropics that its exports amount to $10 billion in 2007, more than sugar and coffee combined.

As if the impacts on the natural environment were not bad enough, there is also the effect on human lives to take into account. Large numbers of agricultural workers have been displaced when their land was taken over for soya production. They have had to look for work elsewhere, leaving their homes behind them. In some cases the land cleared belonged to native tribes who rely on the forest for their existence, as with the Brazilian Enawene Nawe Indians, whose plight was recently highlighted by an International Survival campaign.

How can you help?
• Try to buy only organic soya
• Support World Wide Fund for Nature's (WWF) work on soya
• Support Greenpeace in its campaign against irresponsible soya production
• Look out for any products offering soya from certified sources

LOCALLY GROWN PRODUCE

A lot of the food found on our supermarket shelves has travelled hundreds, if not thousands, of miles to reach us. Our demand for exotic fruits and vegetables all year round means that we are buying more and more imported produce. This not only affects our farmers as they struggle to compete, but also adds to the world's carbon dioxide emissions with the added transport.

If you buy your food locally, you are not only supporting our local economy and growers, but you

SEASONAL FRUIT AND VEGETABLES IN THE UK

Spring	Summer
Asparagus	Asparagus
Broccoli	Aubergine
Brussels sprouts	Beetroot
Carrots	Broad beans
Leeks	Carrots
Lettuce	Cauliflower
Parsnips	Courgettes
Radishes	Cucumber
Spinach	French beans
Spring cabbage	Lettuce
Spring onions	Mangetout
Tomatoes	Onions
Turnips	Peas
Winter cabbage	Potatoes
	Radishes
	Runner beans
	Spinach
	Spring onions
	Summer cabbage
	Sweetcorn
	Tomatoes
	Turnips
	Blackberries
	Blackcurrents
	Cherries
	Cooking apples
	Dessert apples
	Gooseberries
	Peaches
	Pears
	Plums
	Raspberries
	Strawberries

SEASONAL FRUIT AND VEGETABLES IN THE UK

Autumn	Winter
Aubergine	Broccoli
Runner beans	Brussels sprouts
Beetroot	Carrots
Broccoli	Cauliflower
Brussels sprouts	Celery
Carrots	Leeks
Cauliflower	Parsnips
Celery	Red cabbage
Courgettes	Spinach
Cucumber	Swede
French beans	Winter cabbage
Leeks	
Lettuce	
Onions	
Parsnips	
Peas	
Potatoes	
Radishes	
Red cabbage	
Spinach	
Swede	
Sweetcorn	
Tomatoes	
Turnips	
Winter cabbage	
Dessert apples	
Blackberries	
Peaches	
Pears	
Plums	
Raspberries	

are contributing to cutting down on greenhouse gas emissions. There are now more and more farmers' markets where you can buy fruit and vegetables that are in season, and they are fun and sociable places to visit. Another way is to buy through vegetable box schemes, whereby you receive a weekly box of vegetables that are not only freshly harvested but are delivered directly to your door. There are now over 200 organic box schemes running in the UK.

A typical box of fruit and vegetables will cost you between £5 and £15 a week, depending on the demands of your family. If you would like a list of organic box schemes around the UK you can contact the Soil Association or you could ask your local council about schemes run by local allotment gardeners.

It is also worth looking for local produce in your supermarket — several are now beginning to use local suppliers. Although, at first, sourcing local food may not be the easiest of tasks, especially when an abundantly stocked supermarket is close to hand, if we are to tackle the mammoth problem of food transportation then we need to make a start somewhere. One hundred years ago nearly all the food we consumed came from within a 20-mile radius of our homes, but today food has become more and more anonymous and we need to be retaught exactly where it comes from and how it is grown. Food has become a convenience, but we definitely need to stop and think before we pick up that inviting box of strawberries in the middle of winter, and ask ourselves at what cost did it arrive on our shelves.

THE PROBLEM OF PACKAGING

Almost everything we buy at supermarkets today seems to be wrapped in plastic, even vegetables like corn on the cob that have their own protective packaging, seem to be wrapped again. Just stand and study the rows of vegetables on display and imagine just what quantity of plastic finds its way to our landfill sites every single day, and for no real purpose.

Did you know that between a quarter and a third of all domestic waste comes from packaging and much of this is from food? It is becoming a major problem because not only is it difficult to recycle, but also plastic that is contaminated with food is hard to reuse. Fruit juice cartons are a prime example because they are made up of several different layers that are laminated together — card, plastic and foil — making them virtually impossible to recycle.

Remember, a lot of fast food is not only bad for your health but much of the packaging is non-biodegradable.

Although the packaging industry argues that it is essential for health and hygiene reasons, in reality it results from the manufacturers' desire to make a brand more desirable and pleasing to the public eye. What you have to remember is that you are actually paying extra for the packaging. Be honest with yourself, what do you do with the packaging once you have removed the contents — throw it straight in the bin? Although many manufacturers are starting to make efforts to make packaging much lighter and thinner, the number of packaged goods is still increasing. Convenience drinks are one of the main offenders, particularly as they require heavier containers to carry them, and even recycling and refilling needs transport to carry the empties.

As individuals our task is to minimise our consumption of packaged products, even if what is inside is a healthy organic option!

Ironically, the traditional glass milk bottle was a classic example of a system that worked. They were reused and normally only travelled a few miles to their destination and yet this practice has almost become a thing of the past. Returnable glass bottles are definitely the best environmental option, provided of course that the transport distances for this heavy cargo are not too far.

We also pay for all this packaging in another way, by paying higher taxes to cope with all the new landfill sites that are required to cope with our rubbish. These, in turn, add to the pollution and can cause more respiratory illnesses. It is essential that we start today to try and cut down on the amount of rubbish that we throw away. We all need to learn to recycle everything that we can, and this is covered in more detail in the section on Recycling (see pages 91–106).

Although it is still early days, government is starting to sit up and take notice of the packaging problem. More than 100 MPs are backing a campaign against excessive packaging to try and reduce the problem of millions of tonnes of wrappers and cartons being dumped in the nation's dustbins. They are urging manufacturers to cut their use of packaging and calling for people to boycott any packaged goods. Play your part and stop buying that cucumber tightly wrapped in plastic, or four apples neatly packaged in a non-recyclable piece of polystyrene. Can you honestly say to yourself it makes the product taste any better?

CARRIER BAGS

The use of plastic carrier bags is now becoming a major problem and with 500 billion to one trillion being used every year throughout the world, it is no wonder. Many of the larger supermarkets are now offering you 'bags for life' schemes, where you buy one large, durable carrier bag for 10p which should last you several trips. When it wears out the supermarket will replace it free of charge and the old one will be recycled by the supermarket. Some supermarkets also offer the 'penny back' scheme, where they give you 1p off your shopping for every bag you reuse. Some supermarkets also offer instore recycling banks for carrier bags or the option to hand the bags back to the driver if your shopping is delivered to your home.

Of course the best way to contribute is by avoiding plastic bags altogether. Take a jute, canvas or string bag with you when you go shopping. For a start, they are much stronger and they won't dig into your hands when you are carrying your shopping home.

Although carrier bags use 70 per cent less plastic than they did 20 years ago, the majority of them are still made from polyethylene — a type of plastic that is non-degradable. This kind of plastic can take a long time to break down, possibly up to hundreds of years.

Things to do with old carrier bags

- Keep hold of your plastic bags and use them next time you go shopping.
- Find out if your local charity shop needs them for reusing.
- Use them to cover the seat of your bike on a rainy day.
- Use carrier bags as bin liners rather than buying them.
- If you are feeling really creative, cut your old bags into 1-inch strips and then join the strips together to make 'yarn'. You can then use this to knit a new bag which will be far larger and stronger than the original. You will need about 60 carrier bags to make one new one.

A great step forward

The small town of Modbury in Devon hit the news on 1 May 2007 as being the first town in the UK to stop the use of plastic carrier bags. This was not due to some government intervention but was because of a hard battle fought by a local activist, Rebecca Hosking. Single-handedly she started to approach shop owners and asked them to stop using plastic and to sell reusable and biodegradable bags instead. The deal was that if a trader put any product in a bag for a customer, then the bag must not be made of plastic. Everyone pulled together and the project really worked, and now they are hoping they can reduce their plastic packaging in other ways.

Hopefully, other towns and cities will sit up and take note and before long many other places will become carrier bag free. Let Modbury inspire you; if they can do it so can the rest of us.

AEROSOLS

With heightened concerns regarding our environment, people have become more aware of the use of aerosols. We have been constantly warned about the dangers of chlorofluorocarbons (or CFCs) to our environment, but are modern aerosols safe to use?

CFCs are a family of chemical compounds developed back in the 1930s as a safe, non-toxic, non-flammable alternative to dangerous substances like ammonia for the purposes of refrigeration and spray can propellants. Over the years their usage grew enormously, but one of the components that make up CFCs – chlorine – was found to have the potential to destroy large amounts of ozone, allowing harmful levels of ultraviolet radiation to reach Earth.

In the 1970s scientists became concerned about the level of CFCs being released into the atmosphere and today aerosols no longer use CFC propellants. By 1978 the US Environmental Protection Agency banned CFCs and after that only a few spray products were allowed to use CFCs – mainly bronchial inhalers for asthmatics. However, even these were phased out at the turn of the century. Manufacturers had to find alternative propellants which include:

hydrofluorocarbons (HFCs), hydrochlorofluorocarbons (HCFCs) and carbon dioxide. One promising alternative is Polygas, a discovery made by a Scottish scientist. It contains a mixture of carbon dioxide and acetone and is believed to be environmentally sound, less flammable and creates high and more consistent pressure. HFCs or hydrofluorocarbons do not harm the ozone layer but they are highly potent greenhouse gases (from 140 to 12,000 times more potent than carbon dioxide). In addition to this there are possible health hazards to using aerosol sprays. There is always the danger of the can exploding if it gets too hot, and some scientists believe that the inhalation of the propellant or gas can be dangerous, especially to people with allergies and lung or heart disease.

Take all these points into consideration and it makes sense to try to avoid buying any product that comes in aerosol form. If the above information does not put you off then just look at the price; aerosols are far more expensive than a product that comes in a simple container.

HOT DRINKS

Coffee, tea, cocoa and sugar are all products that can be fair traded to the benefit of everyone, and yet this is not normally the case. They are dried goods which do not weigh very much and have a long shelf-life. It would be easy to transport them worldwide with relatively low cost to the environment. However, the majority of our supply comes from places and people that are still being ruthlessly exploited.

Cocoa and slavery

In recent years it has come to light that there is a connection between cocoa farms and child labour in the Cote d'Ivoire, or Ivory Coast, in West Africa. Young boys aged between 12 and 16 have been sold into slave labour and are forced to work in cocoa farms in order to harvest the beans, from which chocolate is made. They are forced to work under inhumane conditions and extreme abuse. The Cote d'Ivoire is one of the leading exporters of cocoa beans to the world markets and discussions have arisen regarding how best to respond to the problem. Most of the boys come from neighbouring Mali, where agents hang around bus stations looking for children who are alone or are begging for food. They lure the kids to travel to Cote d'Ivoire with them, and then the traffickers sell the children to farmers. While we get the pleasure of eating and drinking chocolate, just think, it could possibly be at the expense of child slaves in Africa.

Of course this problem is not isolated to cocoa farms, it affects coffee, tea and sugar plantations as well. Our first choice should be to buy those products that carry a Fair Trade label where we know the producers are receiving a fair price for their product. It also guarantees that no child or forced labour is involved.

Tea bags and coffee filters
When choosing coffee filters try to find ones that are made out of unbleached material. This will make no difference to the final taste of the drink, but it will make a difference to the environmental impact. Bleached coffee filters have been treated with chlorine bleaches which can mean dioxins in the atmosphere and also leave a chlorine residue in your coffee.

Tea bags very often have a skeleton of nylon within the paper sachet to hold them together when they become wet. However, this nylon is non-biodegradable as many home composters have found out. Many organic products use pure paper for their tea bags which are totally biodegradable or, of course, you could go back to using good old leaf tea. If you don't want the bother of making a whole pot of tea for yourself, many specialist tea shops and hardware stores sell single-cup filters just for this purpose.

Decaffeinated coffee and tea

Today, many people drink decaffeinated coffee and tea, especially in the evening when they have found that the caffeine keeps them awake. However, did you know that to make a product caffeine-free the manufacturers have had to use a solvent. The possible solvents are:

- *Methylene chloride*. This is governed by stringent regulations about permitted residue levels due to its toxicity. Some European countries, in particular Germany, strictly control the amount of solvent that escapes into the atmosphere as factory emissions because of the possible damage to the ozone layer.

- *Ethyl acetate*. Although this is marketed as 'natural' decaffeination because ethyl acetate can occur naturally in fruit, there are still concerns regarding the health effects from the solvent residue.

- *Water*. This is a much healthier option, but unfortunately is four times more expensive, a difference that is reflected in the price of the product.

- *Carbon dioxide*. This is pressurised until it becomes a liquid and is considered safe to both the environment and human health.

If you are worried about the type of process that has been used to make your decaffeinated product, why not drink green tea instead. This is made from the same tea leaves but has not gone through the same rigorous processing. It has simply been steamed and dried which gives a lighter flavour and a much lower caffeine content. One word of warning though, women who are trying for a baby should avoid drinking too much of it as it reduces folic acid levels.

Another alternative are herbal teas which have been with us for thousands of years. Some are drunk for their health-giving properties, whilst others are consumed for their refreshing, taste-tingling qualities. Find out where the teas have been produced, for example in the UK or whether they have been transported for great distances. It is best to look for ones that claim to be organically produced.

BOTTLED WATER

One of the most profitable schemes ever thought up to deprive the gullible of their money has to be the sale of bottled water. In the Western world tap water is about as safe as it can get and it is also relatively cheap, so why on earth would you want to spend so much more to obtain it in a bottle?

Did you know that the health and safety standards applied to bottled water are considerably lower than those for regular tap water? Although the label on the bottle of mineral water may claim amazing healing powers, there is no real evidence as to its exact source. Despite the manufacturer's claims it is just as likely that the bottled water came from a very mundane source and possibly industrially contaminated as well.

Not only will you be wasting your money but you are buying unnecessary packaging as well. Added to this is the cost of transporting the product, using unnecessary energy when all you need to do is turn on your tap. The simplest, and greenest, approach if you are going somewhere where you know you will need water but it is difficult to obtain, is to take an empty bottle with you and fill it from the tap before you leave.

If you are really worried about the additives in your tap water, then you can always resort to buying a water filter. Of course the filter will need replacing on a regular basis but you could choose one that is made out of fabric as opposed to the normal plastic cartridge — they are available. Some manufacturers will accept their filters back for recycling which eliminates the problem of throwing away something that is non-biodegradable.

TOILETRIES AND COSMETICS

The cosmetics market has become more environmentally friendly over the last few years, with CFC aerosols and incidents of animal testing being reduced significantly. However, there are still certain brands and chains that should be avoided. The key factors when purchasing a cosmetic product are animal testing and cruelty, rare species as ingredients, and overpackaging. Wherever and whenever possible, when buying cosmetics or toiletry products, follow these simple guidelines:

• Make sure that the product contains natural and non-toxic ingredients;
• Make sure that they have not been tested on animals;

- Make sure that the packaging is kept to an absolute minimum;
- Make sure that the company has an ethical policy towards its workers and operations.

Read the label carefully before purchasing any cosmetics and make sure that they use only natural ingredients to avoid the risk of skin irritation caused by powerful chemicals that could also damage the environment. To minimise the risk of potentially harmful chemicals, it is wise to choose products that are plant-based or marked as 'organic'.

The second priority is the amount of packaging and whether the container can be recycled. Many toiletries, particularly the more expensive ones, are sold in very elaborate packaging to catch your eye. Much of this packaging is completely unnecessary and simply adds to the mountains of rubbish we already throw away. Another point to watch out for is that the packaging itself can be deceptive, often leading the consumer to believe that it holds a lot more than it really does.

As with cleaning products for your home, the first thing you can do is actually reduce the number of different cosmetic products that you buy. It really isn't necessary to have so many choices of cleansers, conditioners, moisturisers, shampoos, toners, etc. Try to stick to simple products, which work just as well and will cost you far less money.

Save money on bath oils by using herbs to scent your water. Rosemary can be used as a conditioner for dark hair, camomile for fair hair, and you can clean your teeth with a mixture of salt and bicarbonate of soda. There are many books available today with recipes for home-made beauty products and you can have fun experimenting as well.

If you are at all worried about any of the ingredients listed on a proprietary brand of toiletry then don't buy it and go and look for a 'greener' alternative.

DETERGENTS

The fragrances contained in many dish and laundry detergents have been known to trigger asthma attacks, headaches and to cause skin and respiratory irritation. You should try to buy detergents that are fragrance-free or those that are plant-based, containing ingredients like coconut oil.

Ecover is a brand that has come onto the market over the past few years and has the added benefit of producing similar chemical-free products for other areas of the house, such as bathroom and kitchen cleaning solutions. Basically, you should be looking for biodegradable solutions that are plant extract based.

Alternatively, see the section on Eco-friendly Cleaning and make up your own solutions.

MEAT AND POULTRY

Since concerns over GM food and processed meat, the sale of organic meat has risen considerably. There is hardly a week goes by that there isn't one chef or another telling us about the atrocities of animals that have been raised in overcrowded, factory-farm conditions. If you want to eat meat or poultry that you know is reared under more natural conditions then you need to consider the organic and/or free range option. Organic meat can be expensive, so you might need to consider eating less to compensate. It is well worth while splashing out on an organic steak, you will certainly notice the difference. Supermarkets now sell a good range of organic products, including meat and poultry, so make sure you can see the word 'organic' on the label. Alternatively, it may say 'Certified Humane Raised and Handled' or 'Free Farmed'. 'Organic' is a government-regulation designation which shows that the animals were raised without using any chemicals or antibiotics.

FISH

Fish can only be labelled 'organic' if it has been raised on a farm, as an EU directive has decreed that nothing captured in the wild can be guaranteed to meet its standards. Organic fish farming is now being readily accepted as it guarantees that the fish are not only fed on uncontaminated food but also the water in which they are raised is not full of pollutants. It also goes towards alleviating the problem of over-fishing and depleted fish stocks.

The main features involved in organic fish farming are:

- No pesticides or chemicals involved in conventional fish farming are used;
- Aquatic ecosystems are maintained;
- The fish are not fed with food containing any artificial colours or GM organisms;
- The farm should promote use of local services.

Free from pollution and any artificial pesticides, organic fish is not only better for you but also tastes far superior. Avoid any fish that has been packaged at the supermarkets as you cannot be certain how it was raised or, indeed, how long it has been standing around before it reaches your table.

One final point to think about at the end of this shopping section is how you travel to and from the shops. Short journeys, especially before the car has warmed up properly, cause the most pollution. If at all possible take to walking, cycling or using public transport for these shorter trips. Not only is it cheaper, the exercise is doing you good as well. One other added bonus is that you won't have to struggle to find a parking space when the car park is busy.

RECYCLING

TOO MUCH RUBBISH

The problem with the world today is that we create too much rubbish and we are running out of places to put it. Each person throws away more than 545 kilograms of rubbish every year and about 80 per cent ends up in landfill sites, or dumps as they are more commonly known. It is estimated that within the next ten years half of the nation's landfill sites will be full and then where will we put our rubbish?

We have been raised with the attitude to throw it in the dustbin and forget about it. No one really wants to think about what happens to it after the dustmen take it away. One of the major problems with the mountains of rubbish that pile up in the dumps is that as the waste decomposes it produces two dangerous substances:

- *methane gas*, which contributes to the greenhouse effect;
- *leachate*, which can seep from older landfills into our water supply causing pollution.

There are currently 2,300 landfill sites in the UK and every day rubbish is transported many miles by large lorries burning lots of fuel and creating even more pollution. It is all a vicious circle.

So what would happen if we solved the problem by burning our rubbish? This sounds like the perfect solution, especially if we could produce energy at the same time, but incineration causes problems of its own. By burning such a vast assortment of items, it would release a range of pollutants into the air including heavy metals, gases that cause acid rain, and gases that contribute to climate change. Also the ash left after the burning can become toxic and would have to be disposed of in landfill sites.

The best way for us to try and alleviate the problem, is to stop thinking about our huge mountains of rubbish as a disposable item and start thinking of ways it could be reused. We need to start taking responsibility for our actions and stop putting future generations at risk. One example are batteries and electronic items which often contain chemicals. If they end up at a landfill site the chemicals will eventually seep to the bottom of the pile and pollute our ground water. This would not only result in contamination of our water but also the soil in which we grow our crops and graze our livestock. The answer to this problem is to teach everyone the IMPORTANCE OF RECYCLING.

- Did you know that you could save enough electricity to power a 100 watt bulb for four hours by simply recycling one single glass bottle?
- Did you know that if you recycle just 1 ton of paper you could be playing your part in producing 31,822 litres (7,000 gallons) of water, 1,727 litres (380 gallons) of oil, and save enough electricity to provide power for your home for six months?

What items can be recycled?
- *Aerosol cans.* Some recycling banks have the facility to recycle aerosols, but you should make sure that the can is empty and that it has not been crushed. Having said that, certain aerosol cans are made from several kinds of plastic and metal and are not suitable for recycling. The safest bet is to avoid buying anything that is packaged in an aerosol can.

- *Aluminium foil*. Aluminium foil should not be put in can banks because it has a different composition, but there are foil banks in certain recycling sites.
- *Batteries*. Ordinary household batteries and the new rechargeable types contain no toxic chemicals. However, rechargeable nickel-cadmium batteries are toxic waste and must be sent back to the manufacturer (many have freepost addresses for this purpose). Silver oxide button cells (the type found in cameras) can be given to jewellers who recover the silver from them. Car batteries should also be returned to the supplier for recycling.
- *Glass*. Glass is made mainly from sand and there is plenty of that in the world. However, the process of turning sand into glass takes an awful lot of energy. It takes a lot less energy to melt glass down to be made into new bottles and jars. Every ton of crushed waste glass can save the equivalent of 136 litres (30 gallons) of oil. The average glass bottle today contains over 25 per cent recycled glass. Green glass bottles manufactured in this country contain sometimes as much as 90 per cent. Glass is one of the main items that are recycled in the UK and in one year alone as much as 500,000 tons of glass can be turned into new products, including fibreglass and building aggregate.
- *Bicycles*. Bicycles are always needed for use in the developing world, so make sure you send your old bike for rehabilitation.
- *Books*. You can take unwanted books to a charity shop, but there is also an internet bookstore called *Greenmetropolis.com* which has been set up specifically to recycle books. It encourages people to buy secondhand books rather than new and, once they have read them, to sell them back so that someone else can read them.
- *Christmas trees*. Because so many Christmas trees

are bought each year — up to five million — it is essential to make sure they are recycled after use. You should contact your local council to find out where to take it so that it can be recycled to become mulch for park flowerbeds. Alternatively, buy a living tree and consider planting it in your garden when you have finished with it.

- *Computers*. There are several establishments now that will collect old computers, revamp them and then supply them to schools and other needy organisations.
- *Drugs*. Take any unused drugs back to the chemist where they will be disposed of safely. Do not pour them down the sink or toilet as they are considered to be hazardous substances.
- *Egg boxes*. Add them to your compost heap or, alternatively, they make perfect seed trays.
- *Furniture*. Instead of taking your old three-piece suite to the dump, why not arrange for it to go to some charitable organisation which can pass it on to someone who may be just setting up home but is struggling to find the money.
- *Green stuff*. Although you should try and compost your green waste at home or take it to your local dump where it will be recycled, many councils now operate a 'green bin' system. Items that can be put out for collection include: grass cuttings, leaves, weeds, dead flowers and plants from the garden, light garden prunings, hedge trimmings, small branches, untreated wood chippings and windfalls of fruit. The reason it is so important to recycle your green waste is because if it goes to a landfill site it will not decompose properly when mixed up with all the other rubbish because it doesn't have access to air. Instead of benefiting the soil it will produce methane which contributes to global warming.

- *Metals* such as aluminium, steel and tin. These are important for two reasons. Firstly, these metals are mined from the ground, which can damage the local landscape and create water and air pollution. Secondly, we can save on this mining if we recycle, because the metals can be melted down and recycled again and again. Twenty recycled aluminium drinks cans can be made with the power it takes to manufacture one brand new one. Recycling 1 kg (2 lb) of aluminium saves 8 kg (17 lb) of bauxite (aluminium ore), 4 kg (9 lb) of chemicals and 14 kWh of electricity.

- *Mobile phones.* There are several schemes in existence that collect and refurbish old mobile phones. For example, Oxfam run the 'bRing bRing' scheme which can turn unwanted phones and their accessories into money to support work with people all over the world. On average, each donated handset is worth £5 to Oxfam.

- *Oil.* Old engine oil can be both messy and hazardous if it is not disposed of properly. Because engine oil can be recycled it should be taken to one of the thousands of oil recycling banks that now have been set up throughout the UK.

- *Paint.* Instead of just throwing away a half-empty tin of paint, why not donate it to an exchange scheme. In this way you will be helping someone who needs paint but is finding it hard to afford.

- *Paper.* Of course, we all know that paper is made from trees and that cutting down too many trees can cause environmental problems. But just imagine how many trees it takes to make all the world's newspapers, magazines, packaging, junk mail, kitchen towels, toilet paper and books to name just a few. It takes at least 25 years for a tree to grow tall enough to be made into paper, something that we throw away every day without giving it a second thought. Producing recycled paper involves up to 70 per cent less energy consumption than making virgin paper and also uses less water. This is because most of the energy used in making paper is in the pulping process needed to turn wood into paper.

- *Plastic.* Plastic is made from chemicals, many of which are made from fossil fuels such as oil. Plastic is one of the hardest items to recycle as there are limited items that it can be turned into. For example, you cannot turn an old hamburger container into another food container. At best it could be used to make a video cassette box, a flower pot or something similar. There are now plastic banks being set up to take plastic drinks bottles but the different types of plastic have so many different properties that recycling is still a problem. Some are made from toxic PVC and are best avoided altogether if at all possible. Those made from PET are fully recyclable, meaning that they can be turned into new bottles. They can also be used to make many other items, from fleece jackets to an assortment of furniture.
- *Printer and toner cartridges.* There are many groups that now provide a recycling service for individuals as well as businesses, with all the proceeds going to charity.
- *Shoes and clothes.* Instead of just throwing away your unwanted clothing and shoes, take them to a charity shop where they can be resold for a worthy cause.
- *Spectacles.* Spectacles are always needed by developing countries and most major opticians will take these off your hands.
- *Televisions.* Fifty per cent of all televisions that are thrown away are found to have only minor faults, or none at all when they have been disposed of to make way for a newer model. Why not donate it to

a hospital, students or other people who can't afford to buy their own television.

- *Tyres*. Some 30 million tyres are scrapped each year: 20 per cent become retreads, 20 per cent are recycled into rubber products and another 10 per cent are exported. The remaining 50 per cent are stockpiled and dumped and some are even disposed of in landfill sites. Many garages and tyre centres now accept old tyres so check with them first before dumping them.

Disposable nappies

Since disposable nappies have become so popular, the disposal of them has become a major problem. Over eight million disposable nappies are discarded into landfill sites every day in the UK. The problem is that they can take anywhere from 200 to 500 years to decompose and it is now estimated that 4 per cent of all landfills are made up of disposable nappies. Just remember, it takes as much energy to produce one disposable nappy as it does to wash a cloth nappy 150 times. Modern technology has made reusable nappies more convenient, unlike the ill-fitting cloth ones of years ago. Today cloth nappies fit better, are patterned with bright colours and can save you a lot of money.

If you really can't stand the thought of going back to reusable nappies, then you might like to consider eco-friendly disposable nappies. They might be a bit more expensive but they are kinder to your baby's skin and to the environment as well.

MAKING YOUR OWN COMPOST

When you consider that 20 to 30 per cent of all your household waste could be used to fertilise your garden, then it is well worth the effort of starting your own compost. Recycle all your plant-based, kitchen and garden waste and when it has rotted down dig it into your soil so that you can have healthy plants and vegetables in a safe, organic way. The finished product is rich, dark, crumbly and sweet smelling. It can be used not only to feed and condition your soil, but also it is great for making potting mixes.

Making compost is often thought to be too complex, but all you need are the right ingredients and simply let nature do the rest.

The first option, and possibly the easiest if you are short of space, is to buy a compost bin. These are generally relatively cheap to buy and are available in wood or recycled plastic (that might otherwise have ended up on a landfill site). It is also possible to buy one cheaply from your local council, so contact your Waste and Recycling Department and start today.

WHAT CAN I COMPOST?
Nitrogen-rich ingredients
- Urine (diluted with water 20:1)
- Comfrey leaves
- Nettles
- Grass mowings
- Raw vegetable peelings from your kitchen
- Tea bags and leaves, coffee grounds
- Young, green weeds (avoid ones that have gone to seed)

- Soft green prunings
- Animal manure from herbivores (e.g. cows and horses)
- Poultry manure and bedding

Carbon-rich ingredients (slow to rot)
- Cardboard (e.g. cereal packets, egg boxes)
- Waste paper and junk mail (ideally, shredded)
- Cardboard tubes
- Newspapers (although it is better to send them for recycling as it is more beneficial to the environment)
- Bedding from vegetarian pets (e.g. rabbits, guinea pigs) — hay, straw, shredded paper, wood shavings
- Hedge clippings
- Woody prunings
- Old bedding plants
- Sawdust and wood shavings
- Fallen leaves

Other items but best used in moderation
- Wood ash
- Hair, nail clippings
- Egg shells (crushed)
- Natural fibres (e.g. wool or cotton)

DO NOT COMPOST (likely to attract vermin and flies)
- Meat
- Fish
- Cooked food
- Coal and coke ash
- Cat litter
- Dog faeces
- Disposable nappies

MAKING YOUR OWN COMPOSTER

If you decide to go down the route of making your own composter you will need the following items:

- Four 1.2 metre (4 foot) high fence posts
- Wire netting or planks
- Galvanised hooks and eyes

Your first job is to clear your compost area approximately 1 square metre (40 square inches), and then use the back of a spade to flatten the soil down. Hammer in the four fence posts at each corner and then either tack wire netting to the posts, or nail planks around them. Leave the front side easily detachable for removing the compost.

The next step is to add some drainage material in the bottom. Put approximately a 10 centimetres (4 inches) layer of coarse material, such as straw or twigs in the base and then build up the sandwich effect. Add a layer of 15 centimetres (6 inches) of garden waste and water if it is too dry. Gradually build up layers of different materials. This layering allows the compost to heat up effectively, and to speed up this process it is an idea to sprinkle a layer of manure or soil in between each layer. This helps to introduce the bacteria or fungi needed to break down the organic material.

When you have completed your pile cover it over with an old piece of carpet, polythene or tarpaulin and leave it for about three months to rot down.

To help add air to the mixture which will make it rot faster, remove the front of your compost box after three months and turn the mixture. Leave it for another three months after which time your compost will be brown, crumbly and sweet smelling and ready to use in your garden.

ADVANTAGES OF A WORMERY

A wormery is a compost bin with a difference — it contains living worms. The difference between a wormery and a regular compost bin is that the liquid that drains from the wormery can be used as a liquid feed. When constructing a wormery you will need to take into consideration the housing needs of the worms and also the type of waste added to benefit the worms.

Compared to regular soil, compost containing worms has:
- 6 times more nitrogen
- 7 times more phosphorus
- 11 times more potassium
- The perfect pH level

To make your wormery you will need a container with a tap at the bottom. You could buy one made especially for the job or, alternatively, use a water butt. Wormeries come in all shapes and sizes and the most popular type is a layered tray structure with a wooden box and a drip tray underneath. This is probably the easiest type to manage, as to harvest the compost you simply have to lift one of the trays out.

If you would like to have a go at making your own you will need:
- your container (water butt and tap or other vessel of your choice)
- a bowl like an old ice-cream container to catch the liquid
- stones

- worms
- bubble wrap
- kitchen scraps and
- probably a good idea — a book about worms

Your first job is to drill holes in the container to allow air to circulate. Collect some large stones and place them in the bottom of the container. This layer needs to be about 15 to 20 centimetres (6 to 8 inches) so that it is deeper than the level of the tap.

Place a layer of compost on top of the stones; this should be approximately the same depth.

Your next job, and your children will love to help you with this part, is to hunt for worms. It is easiest to find worms on damp days as they are more likely to come to the surface. When you find them, take good care of them and do not leave them lying around in the sunlight as they will die. Gather as many as you can and place them directly in a box full of soil or compost. When you feel you have enough, make a dip in the compost layer, add the worms and then cover them up.

Add kitchen scraps so that they have something to start feeding on. As they eat the scraps their urine will drain through the pebbles and you can start to collect it from the tap as liquid feed and, more importantly, it doesn't smell!

When the weather turns cold you will need to keep the wormery warm by bringing it under cover in a shed or, alternatively, wrapping it in bubble wrap. This will help the worms survive the winter and they will continue breeding. Don't forget when you go away on holiday to ask someone to continue feeding them so they don't die.

KERBSIDE RECYCLING

Although it is not in operation in all counties, many councils now offer kerbside recycling. The households taking part in this type of scheme are provided with two wheeled bins — a green one for recyclables and a black one for dirty or non-recyclable waste. These bins are easily moved, help prevent smells and spillage and also look much tidier than the piles of black plastic sacks that used to lay around waiting for collection.

The bins are generally collected on alternate weeks, with the green bin one week and the black the following week. Many councils also offer recycling sacks and blue boxes for paper and plastics, which can be put out at the same time. The householder is given a detailed list of what they can and can't put in their bins.

This type of recycling has already seen a rise in the amount of material being recycled and a considerable reduction in what is being sent to landfill sites.

JUNK MAIL

Unwanted junk mail has grown by 70 per cent since 1998 and it is forecast to continue to grow. Not only is it a nuisance for the householder, it is also a considerable waste of precious paper.

You can of course simply pin a notice on your front door to try and stop the postman pushing unaddressed envelopes and leaflets through your letterbox, but the chances are this won't work. Unfortunately, the Post Office earns millions from delivering advertising material and they won't be put off that easily.

You can stop door-to-door deliveries simply by sending an email to optout@royalmail.co.uk with your name and address, clearly stating that you do not want any more junk mail delivered to your house. Alternatively, if you do not have access to a computer, you can write to your local office asking them to stop sending unaddressed mail to your address.

If you want to stop other forms of unsolicited mail dropping on your doormat, you can register your address with the Mailing Preference Service. Direct mail marketing companies are legally not allowed to target homes that have registered.

Just imagine if everyone registered to stop unwanted junk mail how much paper would be saved. Make it one of your priorities today.

A QUICK REMINDER

- Use your local recycling banks or kerbside collection.
- Find second uses for large items like electronic equipment or furniture. Many towns have projects to distribute such items to those in need (ask your local authority).
- Compost your organic kitchen and garden waste. You may be able to buy a subsidised compost bin from your council.
- Reuse or recycle all types of suitable rubbish, not just packaging. Particularly, you can separate out newspapers, magazines, clothes and junk mail.
- Think about what you buy in your shopping — try to avoid goods with a lot of packaging.
- Reuse bags and boxes for your shopping, reducing the need for new carrier bags.
- Does your retailer offer 'bags for life'?
- Clear out those old clothes and give them to a charity shop (or a younger brother or sister!).
- Reduce the amount of junk mail you receive.
- Could you help a less mobile neighbour to recycle by taking their items to a bank or putting them out on the kerb for collection?
- To fully play your part you should also consider buying products that have a recyclable content.
- Make sure you look for this sign, because then you know that the product you are buying can be recycled.

WATER
FACTS

THE WATER SITUATION

Everyone worldwide needs water and the demand is ever increasing. As hot weather and overuse puts more and more pressure on existing water supplies in vulnerable parts of the country, finding fresh water is getting harder. To start with, the population keeps rising, the British population alone rose by 10 million between 1950 and 2000. It is expectected to continue to grow by 6.1 million to 65.7 million by 2031 before reaching its peak of 67 million around two decades later. With so many more people on the planet, the demands for water for washing, growing food and just sustaining life are growing hour by hour.

The south of England in particular is putting considerable strain on the country's water reserves, as more and more houses are being built. This also puts additional pressure on the environment through the treating and transporting of water all over the country, to where it is needed most.

As we the public demand more water, the water companies are forced to extract more precious water from existing underground reservoirs and rivers. These supplies are not refilled quickly enough due to the dwindling amount of rainfall and this has two major effects:

- Natural habitat is being altered as too much water is being drained away, causing many species of wildlife to suffer — e.g. butterflies, birds and otters.
- Low levels in the rivers increase the risk of pollution because there is less oxygen for the plant and animal life that they normally support.

Rainfall across England in January 2006 was below half the long-term average and rivers and groundwater levels across much of southern England were at a historical all-time low. In fact two rivers in the Thames region, the Ash and the Mimram, had stretches that ran completely dry. Water-saving measures had to be introduced and many homes in the south-east of England had to have some form of hosepipe ban.

Of course the real issue rests with us at home. Each year our demands for water increase and this increase shows no signs of abating whatsoever. We may eventually all be forced to have water meters in our homes so that we can be more aware of the amount of water we are using — or rather wasting!

HOW MUCH DO WE ACTUALLY USE?

You will probably be surprised to learn that:

1 flush of the toilet	3.5–7 gallons
1 bath	25–30 gallons
1 10-minute shower	50–70 gallons
1 washing machine load	25–40 gallons
1 dishwasher load	9.5–12 gallons
Hose or garden sprinkler	240 gallons an hour

If your home is a typical family home, each member uses about 80 gallons of water a day. We all need to try to reduce the amount of water we use and play our part in helping to save our natural resources.

WATER POLLUTION

There are many ways that our precious water becomes polluted, some of which may surprise you. Although you may think that industrial dumping causes the most pollution, you would be incorrect as this only accounts for about 10 per cent contamination.

Because the majority of our water comes from underground sources it picks up whatever it passes through. For example, rainwater and melted snow that runs off roofs, car parks, streets and farms can carry many noxious substances. During a storm many of these pollutants get washed into our rivers and streams and once they get into our water system they never leave.

Farmers are one of the main contributors to this contamination because if they use chemical pesticides and fertilisers, water running off their land pollutes the water supply.

Personal waste items such as tampons, sanitary towels, nappies, cotton buds, condoms and cigarettes can cause blockages in pipes if they are flushed down the toilet. This waste reaches the sewage treatment plants and if they cause a blockage it means that the sewage will eventually end up in our rivers and seas. Try and get into the habit of discarding these items sensibly rather than flushing them down the toilet.

Many chemicals that we use to clean our homes might have an amazing effect but they make a real mess of the water supply when they find their way into the rivers. Detergents contain phosphates which, when released into our lakes and rivers, damage the eco-system and can kill fish and other organisms. Try to find alternative ways of cleaning your home — read the section on Cleaning the Eco-Friendly Way in this book.

WHAT CAN WE DO TO HELP?

Outdoors

We all know that a garden needs water to survive but during a long, hot spell there are ways of keeping your garden blooming and saving water at the same time.

- Water the plants from their roots rather than their leaves. You can do this by cutting off the bottom of a plastic water bottle and inserting it into the soil so that the narrow end is directed straight at the roots. Pour water into the upturned bottle and the water will only go where it is needed.
- Only water plants in the evening after the sun has gone down; this way, less water will evaporate.
- While the soil is still moist apply a layer of mulch (for example fermented grass cuttings) to the surface to hold in the moisture.
- Do not use a sprinkler as it uses too much water.
- Use a seep hose which is available from your water company.
- Fit a trigger gun to the head of your hose; in that way you can turn the water off when you don't need it.
- Try not to cut your lawn too short as longer grass retains moisture for longer. Even if it does turn brown, remember it will soon turn green again when the rain eventually comes.
- Use water butts to collect rainwater from the downpipes connected to the gutters on your house. Rainwater is better for your plants and it is free.

Indoors

- Remember to turn the tap off when you are cleaning your teeth.
- Wash fruit and vegetables in a bowl rather than under a running tap.
- Use a bowl to wash up in rather than the sink as it holds less water.
- Make sure all taps are turned off completely and fix any dripping taps.
- Only use the washing machine when you have a full load. If you have to do a small load use the economy or half-load setting.
- When you buy a new appliance make sure you check the efficiency label — the water consumption should be under 55 litres (12 gallons) per cycle.
- Before taking a bath or shower think about how much water you will be using. Don't overfill the bath and remember that a power shower will use more than a regular shower.
- Fit a water Hippo or eco-flush into your toilet cistern. Every time a toilet is flushed the Hippo saves approximately 3 litres (½ gallon) of water. Check with your water supplier because some authorities give hippos away for free.

CLEANING THE ECO-FRIENDLY WAY

GREEN CLEANING SOLUTIONS

As more and more chemicals hit the shelves of our supermarkets claiming to be a miracle cleaner, those of us who are conscious of the environment are turning more and more to 'green' cleaning. Green cleaning is just a different way of thinking about what you put on the surfaces in your home, what you breathe in and what you touch. I have many friends and relatives who have complained of skin or breathing problems and were convinced that it was down to the products they were using in their home. These people were desperate to try and change their lifestyle, but didn't really know where to begin.

This section gives a few hints and tips on alternative cleaners that won't pollute the atmosphere, our water or ecology. If you already have vinegar, bicarbonate of soda, fresh lemons and olive oil in your house, then you have the basics for green cleaning. There is no need to spend a lot of money on super-tough chemicals, you can muster up your own natural house cleaners from ingredients already in your cupboards.

THE ESSENTIALS

White vinegar
This is a natural disinfectant, stain remover and reduces mineral and lime deposits. This is a great substitute for ammonia-based cleaners and white distilled vinegar costs very little to buy. Added to that it is:
- biodegradable
- easy to dispense and control
- safe for stainless steel

- relatively non-toxic and stable, so safe for handling
- has a pleasant, clean smell
- can be used where environmental considerations are especially important

Bicarbonate of soda

This is a miracle cleaner. When it is mixed with water it forms a slightly alkaline liquid which cuts through grease or dirt on almost any surface. When it is used neat it is slightly abrasive and can be used to scrub problem stains. If you want a really powerful cleaner then you can mix vinegar and bicarbonate of soda together. One word of warning, though, don't use bicarbonate of soda on your non-stick pans as it is likely to damage the surface.

Lemons

Lemon juice is nature's natural bleach and disinfectant rolled into one. Not only is it effective as a stain remover but also a great deodoriser, making it a very efficient and harmless cleaner.

Olive oil

This is a great alternative to furniture polish. Don't worry about buying the extra virgin type, the most basic of brands will do.

GET CLEANING

Ants

If you want to ant-proof your kitchen just give them the lemon treatment. Squeeze lemon juice on door thresholds and windowsills and into any holes or cracks where ants are likely to get in. The ants will soon get the message that they are not welcome.

Aromatic air freshener

Add approximately 15 grams ($^3/_4$ ounce) each of sage, rosemary, mint, rue and wormwood to 570 millilitres (1 pint) of wine or cider vinegar. Allow the herbs to stand in the vinegar for about a week in a warm place. Strain and use as an air freshener or to control unpleasant smells.

Baby bottles

These can be cleaned with a solution of bicarbonate of soda and water. Make sure you rinse them thoroughly.

Biodegradable bug and fly spray

Spraying bugs inside the home means that you get chemicals on carpets and furniture. Try filling an old water pistol with vinegar and you can spray the offending insect without damaging the decor.

Bloodstains

Soak clothing in a bucket of cold water with a cup of vinegar and an equal amount of bicarbonate of soda. Leave overnight before washing as normal.

Brighten whites

To brighten whites that can't be bleached, just pour a small amount of lemon juice into the washing machine at the start of the wash cycle.

Brighter stainless steel

Spots on your stainless steel or aluminium kitchen equipment can be removed by rubbing with white vinegar.

Burnt-on food

To remove stubborn burnt-on food from a pan, fill it with warm water, add lemon slices and allow it to simmer for about 15 minutes or until the food starts to break loose from the surface.

Chopping boards
Wipe down chopping boards with full strength vinegar. It will clean and disinfect them, cut grease and absorb odours.

Alternatively, you can rub the board all over with the cut side of half a lemon or wash it in undiluted lemon juice.

Dentures
Instead of soaking your dentures in harmful chemicals, why not soak them in vinegar for as long as you would leave them in a regular denture cleaner. Then brush them thoroughly.

Dishwasher powder
Instead of using a commercial brand of dishwashing detergent, try mixing two tablespoons of bicarbonate of soda with two tablespoons of borax for a load.

Disinfectant
Anywhere you want to kill germs, whether in the kitchen or the bathroom, apply a liberal mixture of vinegar and water.

Dog bath and flea control
Adding a little white vinegar and bicarbonate of soda to a bath will make your dog less 'doggy' and also leave it with a soft, shiny coat.

Drain cleaner
Vinegar and bicarbonate of soda cause a chemical reaction when combined, so be prepared. They break down fatty acids from grease, other foods and a

build-up of soap into simpler substances. Pour 50 grams
(2 ounces) of bicarbonate of soda and 150 millilitres
($1/4$ pint) of vinegar into the drain. Cover if possible
while the solution fizzes. Follow this with a bucketful
of very hot water.

Dustbins
Sprinkle half a tub of bicarbonate of soda into the
bottom of the empty dustbin. Swill round with a
couple of bowls of warm water and leave for a while.
Empty out down the nearest drain.

Fabric softener
White vinegar in the softener compartment of your
washing machine softens laundry beautifully.

Floor cleaner
Add 150 millilitres ($1/4$ pint) vinegar to 4.5 litres
(1 gallon) of water to keep your vinyl floors clean and
shining.

Fridge
Bicarbonate of soda mixed with water is ideal for
cleaning the inside of your fridge, because not only
will it cut through greasy marks but it eliminates
those nasty niffs as well.

Fridge freshener
Dab lemon juice onto a piece of cotton wool or
sponge and leave in the fridge for several hours or
overnight.

Grass/weedkiller
Kill unwanted weeds or grass with a direct application
of vinegar on the trouble spot.

Hand cleaner

Remove cooking smells from your hands by rinsing them with vinegar and then washing thoroughly with soap and water.

Hard water deposits

Use vinegar to get rid of hard water deposits around your sink. Soak paper towels in vinegar and place them around the area that needs to be cleaned. For cleaning the tap you can soak the towel, wrap it around and then use a rubber band to keep it in place. Do this overnight and by the morning they will be easy to wipe clean. This is also safe for brass taps.

Ink stains

To remove ink stains from fabric, apply lemon juice liberally while the ink is still wet. Then wash the garment with a little detergent in cold water.

Kitchen bin

Use a fairly strong solution of bicarbonate of soda and water to wash your kitchen bin; this also helps to keep smells away. Safe for plastic and stainless steel.

Leather upholstery

Leather can be revived by wiping with a damp cloth sprinkled with a little white vinegar.

Limescale

Pour a cup of white vinegar into your kettle, leave overnight then in the morning boil up with water. Pour out water and limescale, refill the kettle, boil again and the kettle will be completely limescale and vinegar free.

Melting snow and ice

Instead of using salt on your garden path, which will

harm any plants it comes into contact with, use bicarbonate of soda to melt snow and ice.

Metal Polishing

Brass: Mix $\frac{1}{2}$ tsp salt and $\frac{1}{2}$ cup white vinegar with enough flour to make a paste. Apply thickly. Leave for 15 minutes to half an hour. Rinse thoroughly with water to avoid corrosion.

Copper: Polish with a paste of lemon juice and salt.

Silver: Boil silver 3 minutes in 1 quart ($\frac{1}{4}$ gallon) of water containing: 1 teaspoon baking soda, 1 teaspoon salt, and a piece of aluminium foil. Or, rub silver with a baking soda/water paste and a soft cloth; rinse and polish dry. Or, rub with toothpaste. Use a toothbrush to clean raised surfaces. Be careful not to scratch surfaces. Be gentle and use a light touch.

Chrome: Wipe with vinegar, rinse with water, then dry. (Good for removing hard water deposits.) Or, shine chrome fixtures with baby oil and a soft cloth.

Stainless steel: Clean and polish with a baking soda/water paste or a cleanser.

Microwave

To clean a microwave oven all you need to do is put a couple of tablespoons of vinegar in a bowl with a cup of water. Microwave on high for 45 seconds to 1 minute and then remove the bowl and wipe out the oven. Any baked-on splatters will be softened and easily removed.

Another method is to mix 3 tablespoons of lemon juice into 400 millilitres ($\frac{3}{4}$ pint) of water in a bowl. Microwave on high for 5 to 10 minutes, allowing the steam to condense on the inside of the microwave. Then simply wipe away the residue food with a cloth.

Nappies

If you decide you would like to go back to using terry nappies to help with the problem that disposable nappies cause, then soak them in a bucket of bicarbonate of soda solution overnight. When you come to wash them you won't need to use such hot water or so much detergent to get them clean and white.

Oil paintings

Rub half a potato on a dirty oil painting to remove grime. This is not recommended for your valuable Renoir; seek professional advice!

Plastic shower curtains

To prevent mildew from forming on plastic shower curtains, keep a spray bottle of vinegar and water in the bathroom and use regularly.

Rust stains

Rust stains can be removed by rubbing with a solution of lemon juice and salt. Leave for a few hours and then wash as normal.

Scratches on furniture

Rub half a walnut into scratches on dark polished wood furniture this will remove the mark completely.

Shower head

Clean a shower head by unscrewing it to remove the rubber washer. Place the head in a pot filled with equal parts vinegar and water and bring to the boil. Simmer for 5 minutes. Alternatively, soak the shower head in vinegar overnight, then rinse in hot water.

Smear-free glass

Put white vinegar and water into a spray bottle for

cleaning glass and windows. Use sparingly and wipe off with newspaper for amazing results.

Sparkling glasses

A few drops of vinegar added to your rinse water will keep your glasses sparkling and water-spot free.

Tea and coffee stains

An equal mixture of salt and white vinegar will clean coffee and tea stains from china cups.

Tiles and grouting

This gives instant results and a sense of extreme satisfaction. Using an old toothbrush and a paste made of two parts bicarbonate of soda to one part white vinegar, rids the grout of the dull build-up in the shower area. Rinse with the shower head for quick results.

Toilet cleaner

Remove stubborn stains by spraying them with vinegar and brushing vigorously. Deodorise the bowl by adding 570 millilitres (1 pint) of distilled vinegar. Allow it to remain for half an hour before flushing.

Alternatively, you can try putting bicarbonate of soda down the pan. Leave for a while before flushing.

Vacuum cleaner

To freshen your vacuum cleaner, place a few drops of lemon juice into the bag just beore you start your chores.

Whitener

For a washing whitener, mix one part lemon juice with one part bicarbonate of soda. Add to your whites for a mild bleaching effect.

Wooden floor cleaner
To clean wooden floors that haven't been varnished, wash them with a solution of lemon juice and water. Not only will your room smell nice but the floor will look amazing too.

Worktops
For stubborn stains on marble, plastic or Formica, make a strong paste of bicarbonate of soda with water. Scour gently and rinse thoroughly.

THE POWER OF OZONE

When most people hear the word 'ozone' they think of a substance that exists in the stratosphere playing a part in controlling global warming. However, ozone is probably one of the most misunderstood chemicals in our daily environment.

Like many other materials, when ozone is discharged into the environment it can cause major problems. However, if it is harnessed and focused for a particular use, it can be a very beneficial and powerful material.

Chemical process industries have recognised the power of ozone for many years and, believe it or not, it is being used widely in a variety of industrial and commercial applications. These include water treatment and waste and waste waters including sewage. Breweries have also used ozone for many years to purify the water used to make beer. It is also used extensively in industries where the destruction of microbial organisms is paramount, hospitals being a prime example.

Ozone is the second most powerful oxidant after fluorine gas and is almost one and a half times stronger than chlorine as an oxidant. If harnessed correctly, ozone can act as a powerful disinfectant which is much faster and more effective than chlorine against many viruses and micro-organisms. It is the strong oxidising power of ozone that causes the problems in our atmosphere, but it is precisely this same power that can be controlled and used in commercial and industrial applications.

Ozone is a very unstable gas and quickly returns to oxygen with the release of an enormous amount of energy. For this reason it cannot be transported and stored so it has to be generated at the site where it is to be used.

OZONE AS A CLEANER

Ozone is more effective as a cleaner than chlorine and leaves no residuals other than oxygen. It can provide superior cleaning with allergen and odour control as well as many other benefits. Because ozone is so strong it only requires small amounts in comparison to chlorine and other oxidants. Also, due to its high reactivity, ozone is toxic to living organisms such as bacteria, moulds and viruses, and in controlled conditions it acts as an invaluable cleaning aid, deodoriser, purifier and micro-biocide. For this reason ozone systems have been approved by all the necessary food governing agencies and it is hoped that we will eventually be able to eliminate the use of chemicals in food processing.

Ozone has also been used effectively as a cleaning agent to help improve health in low income housing, where high levels of asthma and other breathing-related illnesses were found to be extraordinarily high. The ozone-assisted cleaning system was used to clean fabrics including upholstered furniture, carpets and mattresses. This helped to reduce cockroach and pest infestations and removed many of the allergens causing the respiratory problems.

At present few hospitals are using the innovative new cleaning system which could dramatically cut numbers of potentially fatal bugs, such as *clostridium difficule* (C diff). This is due to the fact that they are being hampered by NHS red tape despite the fact that scientists have proved that standard laundry systems that use detergents and very hot water do not kill the superbug. The new ozone technology uses detergent-free cold water which is subjected to high voltage electricity, which creates the ozone gas. Hopefully the restrictions will soon be lifted as it is known that ozone acts 3,200 times faster than chlorine bleach and is a lot kinder to the environment.

GROWING
YOUR OWN

GROWING YOUR OWN

Imagine walking into your garden or your allotment and picking a basket of fresh vegetables and, less than a couple of hours later, they are on your plate. The taste of fruit and vegetables freshly picked is far superior to produce bought at the supermarket which may have been sitting around for a long time before it reaches your table. This part of the book aims to give you a simple guide to the advantages of starting your own organic garden.

The aim of organic gardening is to create an environment in which healthy plants can be grown successfully without the aid of chemicals that would either pollute the soil or damage wildlife. If you create an environment like this, then natural predators will do the work for you, alleviating the need to artificially control pests and diseases.

GETTING TO KNOW YOUR SOIL

First and foremost it is important to stress that soil is our planet's most valuable asset, so we need to learn to treat it with the utmost respect.

If you are one of those people who are lucky enough to start off with a good fertile soil, then you are already well on the way to your organic garden. However, if like a lot of us you are not so lucky and your soil is sandy or rich in clay, then you have a lot more work to do.

Soil falls into five general groups — clay, loam, sand, chalk and peat — but it would be fair to say that most gardens have a mixture of soils, with one type predominating. To be able to cultivate your soil to its best advantage you will need to decide what type of soil you have. Watch carefully when it rains — if water takes a long time to drain away then it is likely you have a clay soil. This type of soil will also be rock hard in periods of dry weather.

If water drains away within minutes even after a heavy downpour, then you most probably have light, sandy soil. Although sandy soil is easy to work with because it is light and free-draining, it will need frequent watering as it quickly runs out of nutrients. If you are plagued with clay, then the opposite is true. Although you will never have a problem with a shortage of nutrients, digging is difficult and you may well have a problem with slugs.

If water drains away fairly quickly after heavy rain but the ground remains unworkable for a couple of days, then you have a soil rich in loam. If speedy drainage is combined with a surface that appears dusty white or grey then you have chalky soil.

Don't give up at the first hurdle, there are ways round poor soil conditions. The answer is to add as much organic matter to the soil as you can get your hands on. Ideally, your own matured compost should be used, but if you do not have enough then there are plenty of choices at your local garden centres. Alternatively, a visit to your local farm or equestrian centre should come up trumps.

By adding decayed wastes to your soil you will be nourishing it with countless microscopic bacteria. It is estimated that there are as many as five billion in one teaspoon of soil, plenty of food for your hungry plants.

As covered in an earlier section, it doesn't matter how large or small your garden is, you can always make room for a compost bin. True organic gardeners are habitual recyclers and don't waste anything. Make sure you make a path leading up to your compost so that you have easy access for your wheelbarrow.

NATURAL CONTROL OF PESTS

Known by a variety of names — blackfly, greenfly, cabbage aphids, etc. — pests can cause a lot of damage by feeding on the sap of young shoots. Now that we know that chemical pesticides are bad for the environment we need to find other ways of deterring pests from destroying our precious crops. This is where recycling comes in handy and why a gardener never throws anything away. Listed below are a variety of organic alternatives to control garden pests without a chemical in sight:

- Offcuts of carpet underlay can be placed around cabbages to stop rootflies from laying their eggs next to the stem.
- Plastic bottles with their bottoms cut off can be placed over plants to confuse slugs.
- Old CDs hung on pieces of string to swing in the breeze will deter birds.
- Lay planks or boards between your rows of vegetables — snails will gather underneath and then you can pick them off daily.
- Aphids can be removed by rubbing with a small brush or your fingers, while caterpillars can be picked off by hand.

- Barrier bands wrapped around the trunk of trees will help prevent insects from reaching the fruit and leaves. Make the band from a piece of old cotton sheet and change regularly to dispose of catch.
- Snail traps. Mix up one part beer to two parts water and then add a little brown sugar. Pour into a saucer sunk into the soil so the lip is level with the ground and remove the snails daily. Alternatively, fill an old bottle with the same mixture and sink to ground level.
- Chives can be grown throughout the garden and act as an insect repellant. You can also make up a garden spray by steeping a handful of chives in boiling water for an hour.
- Herbs act as a natural insect repellant so it is worth planting them throughout your vegetable patch.

Caterpillars can be easily picked off by hand, but make sure that you wear gloves.

- Plain old hot water has a fatal effect on many insects. Soft bellied insects cannot survive temperatures of 45°C (113°F) and beetles will die at 54°C (129°F). Even the most delicate plant will not be damaged by these temperatures.
- Marigolds are excellent repellants, plant them throughout your garden and the pungent secretions will ward off many harmful insects.
- Milk is a versatile garden spray so make up a simple solution of one part milk to two parts water.
- Onions are also an effective repellant. Pour 500 millilitres (1 pint) of boiling water over 1 kilogram (2 pounds) of chopped onion and allow it to stand for 24 hours. Strain and dilute with 20 litres (5 gallons) of water. This is particularly good for the control of sucking insects like aphids, thrips and mites. To use pour around each of the affected plants and repeat every two weeks until clear.
- White pepper dusted on your vegetables will help keep caterpillars at bay.
- Salt can be sprinkled directly onto pests or used as a spray, again particularly good for caterpillars and slugs.
- Pure soap is an essential ingredient in many sprays. If you mix it with 9 litres (2.3 gallons) of water in a spray bottle it is an effective way to control both aphids and caterpillars.
- Washing soda is a great deterrent against fungi and mildew. Mix 250 grams (9 ounces) of washing soda with 11 litres (3 gallons) of water and 125 grams (4 ounces) of soft soap. DO NOT use this mixture in very hot weather as it can burn the plant.
- Garlic is renowned for its insecticidal properties. Make up a good all-round spray by soaking 50 g (1½ ounces) of chopped garlic with one tablespoon of mineral oil and 250 millilitres (½ pint) of water.

Allow the mixture to stand for 48 hours and then strain.

Perhaps the best way to control insect pests is to encourage natural predators into your garden. If you have room, dig a pond to encourage frogs and toads; they enjoy a tasty meal of slugs. Ideally, it needs to have varying depths and at least one side sloping up gradually so that the frogs have an easy access. Toads don't spend as much time as frogs do in the water, but they love nooks and crannies to hide in.

A plentiful supply of mulch will encourage beetles and spiders, both of whom will make life difficult for pests that try to live in the soil.

Encourage birds to stay near your garden by planting some leafy bushes and trees. Shrubs with berries in winter are great winter food for the birds and if they get used to coming into your garden they will love to help you with your pest control.

Encourage hedgehogs by leaving some scrub and leaf litter under sheltered hedges and in dark corners. Leave out a bowl of water as hedgehogs suffer in periods of drought and they will reward you by eating your slugs. You could also build a simple hedgehog house using two large paving stones sandwiched together with bricks. Then fill the space with a mixture of straw and leaves.

Ladybirds and lacewings adore eating aphids so find out from your local garden centre which plants will attract them or see page 135.

FORMING THE CHAIN OF LIFE

Having attracted all these natural predators into your garden then you are supporting nature's natural chain of life. Plants, animals and soil all interact to make up the basic cycles of nature. As you increase the life in your organic soil then that in itself goes on to support larger forms of life not only in your garden but in the surrounding environment as well. After all, if you want birds then you have to have worms. Once again the effects are cumulative. As more wildlife visits your garden they bring with them nutrients and minerals that further enhance the fertility of your soil. For example, birds shed their feathers, drop eggshells, nesting material and copious droppings, all of which are regenerated in the soil.

Creatures such as frogs, toads, rabbits and hedgehogs also take part in this same process and all give off precious carbon dioxide which is reabsorbed by your garden plants. Although we keep going on about the dangers of too much carbon dioxide in our atmosphere, what you have to realise is that it is vital for plant growth. In the carbon cycle, plants absorb carbon dioxide from the atmosphere and use it to their advantage, combined with the water they get from the soil. The process of photosynthesis (conversion of sunlight into energy) incorporates the carbon atoms from carbon dioxide into sugars. Animals, such as a rabbit, eat the plants and then use the carbon to build up their own tissues. Other animals, such as the fox, eat the rabbit and then use the carbon for their own needs. These animals return carbon dioxide into the air when they breathe and into the soil when they die, through decomposition, and so the carbon cycle continues as a new plant absorbs the carbon atoms in the soil.

PLANTS THAT ARE BENEFICIAL TO INSECTS AND WILDLIFE

Plant	Wildlife
Borage	Bees
Buddleia	Lacewings, butterflies
Campanula	Bees
Candytuft	Butterflies
Catnip	Bees, butterflies
Chives	Bees, butterflies
Clover	Bees
Cosmos	Lacewings, bees, hoverflies
Cranesbill	Birds
Dill	Hoverflies
Fennel	Hoverflies, bees, ladybirds
Forget-me-not	Bees
Goldenrod	Hoverflies, bees, lacewings
Honesty	Butterflies, birds
Honeysuckle	Bees, butterflies
Lavender	Bees
Lovage	Hoverflies
Marigold	Hoverflies
Marjoram	Bees, butterflies
Meadowsweet	Birds
Mint	Bees, butterflies
Poached egg plant	Hoverflies, bees
Rosemary	Bees
Scabious	Butterflies
Sweet cicely	Hoverflies
Sunflower	Bees, butterflies, birds
Teasel	Bees, butterflies, birds
Thyme	Bees
Valerian	Bees, butterflies
Yarrow	Lacewings, bees, ladybirds, hoverflies

THE IMPORTANCE OF POLLINATORS

By growing a wide variety of plants in your garden you will attract many beneficial insects and wildlife (see chart on page 135). Pollinators are essential to our environment and the ecological service they provide is necessary for the reproduction of nearly 70 per cent of the world's flowering plants. Bees are the best known pollinators, but of course hoverflies, butterflies, flies, beetles and wasps all visit flowers and pollinate them. Beetles are good pollinators in cold wet conditions when other insects cannot fly.

Flowers have many tricks up their sleeves to attract pollinators to ensure their own reproduction. Their beautiful colours, interesting shapes and fascinating scents have only one purpose and that is to attract pollinators.

Fruits and seeds derived from insect pollination are a major part of the diet of approximately 25 per cent of all birds.

In many parts of the world, however, the esssential service of pollination is at risk due to loss of natural habitat, alteration and fragmentation, as well as the use of uncontrolled pesticides. By having an organic garden you are ensuring that the essential job of pollination continues to provide economic and ecological benefits to humans, flowering plants and wildlife. Make sure you play your part in preserving these important environmental components.

NATURAL RECYCLERS

We should take our lead from nature's natural

recyclers as every living thing depends on absorbing pieces of other dead creatures in order to survive. Plants build up their materials from air, light, water and the breakdown of other produce. The faster the rate of turnover and the more forms of life we can encourage into our garden, the more it will reward us and supply us with fresh produce. Most of nature's natural recyclers (such as beetles, snails, etc.) live on or in the soil. Without these recyclers our world would be filled up with a lot of nasty, smelly little corpses. These recyclers convert dead and diseased material back into life in the form of plant food. Once the matter is broken down and digested to become droppings, it goes back into the soil and acts as a fertiliser. This process works best in damp, warm conditions and if we supply organic mulch the natural recyclers will rapidly convert it into fertile matter.

Make sure you do your best to create a garden that will attract as much wildlife as possible.

PLANTING SEASONS

Start today to create your own natural, organic garden, a sustainable environment for you and your family to enjoy. The next few pages are a guideline in how to work your garden month by month. Correct timing is vital for the successful growing of fruit and vegetables so use the guide for when to sow or plant, when to prune, which fertiliser to use and general hints on cultivation. You will need to take into account the vagaries of a particular season, but I have based my calendar on an 'average' year in the south of England.

When looking at seed packets it can sometimes be confusing as to when the seasons start and end, so I have given a rough guide to which months relates to which season.

Early Spring	March
Mid Spring	April
Late Spring	May
Early Summer	June
Mid Summer	July
Late Summer	August
Early Autumn	September
Mid Autumn	October
Late Autumn	November
Early Winter	December
Mid Winter	January
Late Winter	February

MID WINTER

PRUNE — Remove damaged or diseased growths only.
PLANT — Chit seed potatoes on trays in a light, frost-free place.
FEED — Spread lime or calcified seaweed on soil every few years.

LATE WINTER

SPRAY — Outdoor peaches and almonds using Bordeaux mixture.
Bordeaux mixture is a fungicidal suspension of copper sulphate and slaked lime. Although it is an inorganic chemical it is allowed under organic standards as it is not harmful to us or the soil.

PRUNE — Removed damaged or diseased growths only.
PLANT — Garlic, onion sets, shallots, shrubs, trees and soft fruit.
FEED — Spread seaweed on grass, bare soil and mulches and rake in.
SOW (under cover in warm) — Indoor tomatoes, early peas, broad beans, cabbages, cauliflower, lettuce, spinach, turnips, carrots, radishes, potatoes.
SOW (under cover in pots) — Onions, spring onions, sweet peas.
TURF — Cut grass on high setting in mild conditions.

EARLY SPRING

SPRAY — Everything with a diluted seaweed solution; outdoor peaches and almonds with Bordeaux mixture.
PRUNE — Less hardy and hollow-stemmed shrubs such as buddleias. Remove old canes of autumn-fruiting raspberries. Cut back evergreens and conifer hedges.
PLANT — Garlic, onions, shallots, artichokes, asparagus, potatoes, evergreens, shrubs, trees, grapevines, soft fruit, rhubarb.
FEED — Spring greens with comfrey liquid or seaweed solution; grassed areas with sieved compost, seaweed or diluted urine.
MULCH — Spread mulches under and around everything possible.
SOW (under cover in warm) — Tomatoes, cucumbers, aubergines, peppers.
SOW (outside in warm soil or under cover) — Peas, broad beans, leeks, beetroot, kohl rabi, cabbages, cauliflowers, lettuce, spinach, turnips, carrots, chards, salsify, scorzonera, parsnips, herbs, radishes, spring onions, sweet peas.
TURF — Cut grass weekly once it is growing fast.

MID SPRING

SPRAY — Everything with a diluted solution of seaweed.

PRUNE — Cut back most early flowering shrubs once flowers die. Remove seed heads from bulbs as they die back.

PLANT — Potato sets, onion seedlings, perennial herbs, evergreens.

FEED — Top dress all permanent container plants with compost.

MULCH — Spread mulches under and around everything possible.

SOW (under cover in warm) — Tomatoes, ridge cucumbers, gherkins, melons, courgettes, marrows, pumpkins, sweetcorn, half-hardy flowers.

SOW (outside and under cover) — peas, broad beans, French beans, runner beans, most brassicas, lettuce and salad plants, herbs, spinach, turnips, carrots, swedes, salsify, radishes, kohl rabi, fennel, leeks, parsnips, sweet peas.

TURF — Cut the grass weekly using the clippings for mulch.

LATE SPRING

SPRAY — Everything with a diluted seaweed solution.

PRUNE — Remove crowded and ill-placed shoots on fruit trees. Cut back most flowering shrubs once flowers die. Tie in and support growing climbers and tall herbaceous plants.

PLANT OUT — Sweetcorn, ridge cucumbers, courgettes and marrows under cover or in open once last frost is well past.

FEED — Incorporate compost with all transplants this month. Feed tomatoes and pot plants with comfrey liquid or seaweed solution.

MULCH — Spread mulches under and around potatoes.
SOW (under cover outside) —Tomatoes, ridge
cucumbers, gherkins, melons, courgettes, marrows,
pumpkins, sweetcorn, half-hardy flowers.
SOW (outside without cover) — Peas, broad beans,
French beans, runner beans, most brassicas, lettuces
and salad plants, herbs, spinach, turnips, carrots,
swedes, salsify, radishes, kohl rabi, fennel, leeks,
parsnips, sweet peas, wallflowers.
TURF — Cut the grass weekly using clippings for mulch.

EARLY SUMMER

SPRAY — Everything with a diluted seaweed solution.
PRUNE — Deadhead and cut back most flowering
shrubs once flowers die. Summer prune grapes and
redirect new growth.
PLANT — Transplant brassica and leek plants.
FEED — Incorporate compost with all transplants this
month. Feed tomatoes and pot plants with comfrey or
seaweed solution.
MULCH — Spread mulches under and around potatoes.
SOW — Lettuces and salad plants, beetroot, kohl rabi,
swedes, turnips, spinach, chicory, endive, biennial
and perennial flowers.
TURF — Cut the grass weekly using clippings for
mulch.

MID SUMMER

SPRAY — Everything with a diluted seaweed solution.
Spray maincrop potatoes with Bordeaux mixture if
warm and humid.
PRUNE — Plums and flowering and fruiting cherries.
Summer prune apples, pears, red and white currants
and grapes. Keep on deadheading. Cut back
evergreens and conifer hedges.

PLANT — Potato sets for late crop.
FEED — Incorporate compost with potato sets.
SOW — Lettuces and salad plants, carrots, swedes,
turnips, Chinese cabbage, winter spinach, kohl rabi,
chards.
TURF — Cut the grass as needed and use clippings for
mulch.

LATE SUMMER

SPRAY — Everything with a diluted seaweed solution.
PRUNE — Cut oldest blackcurrant stems back hard
after fruit is harvested.
PLANT — Daffodil bulbs, transplant rooted strawberry
runners.
SOW — Winter lettuces and salad plants, Japanese
and spring onions, winter spinach, green manures as
soil becomes vacant.
TURF — Cut the grass if needed and use clippings as
mulch.

EARLY AUTUMN

SPRAY — Everything with a diluted seaweed solution.
PRUNE — Cut back herbaceous plants to
15 centimetres (6 inches) as the stems wither.
Remove old canes and tie in new for raspberries and
blackberries.
PLANT — Garlic and other bulbs. Transplant biennial
flowering plants.
FEED — Incorporate compost with all transplants this
month.
SOW (under cover) — Winter lettuces and salad
plants, early carrots, turnips, Chinese greens.
TURF — Cut the grass if needed and use clippings for
mulching.

MID AUTUMN

PRUNE — Late-flowering shrubs, soft fruit and grapes as leaves fall. Cut back herbaceous plants to 15 cm (6 in) as the stems wither. Remove old canes and tie in new for raspberries and blackberries.
PLANT — Garlic and other soft bulbs. Deciduous shrubs, trees and soft fruit.
FEED — Incorporate compost with all plantings this month. Spread sieved compost around trees, shrubs and soft fruit.
MULCH — Spread mulches under and around everything possible.
SOW (under cover) — Winter lettuces and salad plants, summer cauliflower, sweet peas, green manures in greenhouse and polytunnel.
TURF — Cut the grass weekly, raising height and returning clippings with shredded leaves or collect them together for mulching.

LATE AUTUMN

PRUNE — Late-flowering shrubs, soft fruit and grapes as leaves fall. Cut back herbaceous plants to 15 cm (6 in) as the stems wither. Rework and winter prune apples, pears and non-stone fruits.
PLANT — Deciduous shrubs, trees and soft fruit.
FEED — Incorporate compost with all plantings this month. Spread compost on top of asparagus and globe artichokes.
MULCH — Spread mulches under and around everything possible.
SOW — Hardy peas and broad beans for extra early crop.
TURF — Cut grass if needed and collect cuttings with leaves for mulching.

EARLY WINTER

PRUNE — Late-flowering shrubs, soft fruit and grapes as leaves fall. Rework and winter prune apples, pears and non-stone fruits.
PLANT — Deciduous shrubs, trees and soft fruit.
FEED — Incorporate compost with all plantings this month. Spread compost on top of crowns of herbaceous plants.
TURF — Lime the grass, aerate and spike if needed, adding sharp sand.

GREEN MANURE

There will probably be periods when an area of your garden or allotment is not in production, for example just after harvesting a crop. The best solution is to cover the area with a thick mulch or compost, or cover with an old carpet to prevent weeds from germinating. The compost will be drawn into the soil by the worms, alleviating the need to dig it in the following spring. Another use for a fallow area is to grow a green manure. This is an annual crop such as mustard (spring or summer sowing) or alfalfa (late summer or autumn slowing). This will prevent soil erosion, smother the weeds and turn the soil — roots and all — so that they are completely buried and will break down, returning the vital nutrients into the soil. Bear in mind though that the soil structure is better maintained when it is being used; a plot that is left barren with nothing growing on it will soon become compacted and stagnant and it will take a lot of extra work to make it fit for planting.

Hopefully this section has given you a few helpful tips and you are now ready to tackle your first organic garden, however small.

REDUCING YOUR CARBON FOOTPRINT

WAYS TO REDUCE
YOUR CARBON FOOTPRINT

This last section is a list of ways that you can help the planet and reduce your own carbon footprint. A carbon footprint is the measure of carbon dioxide that goes into the atmosphere as you go about your day to day life. Almost every single thing you do affects it, from making a cup of coffee, to buying food and driving your car. Air travel accounts for about 3.5 per cent of human contribution to global warming and if your job involves a lot of travelling you might wonder what you can do about it. The good news is that you can OFFSET your carbon footprint by making other choices — for example trying to cut down on the number of times you use your car. Many people struggle with this and wonder whether the tiny part they play can really make a difference. Of course it can; imagine if we all said the same thing! Start today by playing just a small part — reuse canvas shopping bags, walk into town and take shorter showers.

Beside each suggestion is a tick box ☑ so that you can keep track of exactly how much you have achieved. Start off by only doing those things that you feel comfortable about, and gradually you will find it easier and easier to make a big difference to the way you live.

☐ **ABANDON THE CAR**
Try leaving your car at home for one journey a week. This will help cut pollution and reduce your level of carbon dioxide emissions. Try walking or cycling to work if possible and get fit at the same time.

☐ ALUMINIUM CANS
Collect aluminium cans and then sell them to a local aluminium recycler. You could buy yourself something nice or even donate the money to a worthy environmental cause.

☐ AVOID AIR TRAVEL
Where possible try to avoid travelling by air. Aircraft currently cause about 3.5 per cent of global warming from all human activities. In 1990 aircraft released more than 600 million tonnes of carbon dioxide into the atmosphere so imagine how much is being released today.

☐ BED
Put an extra blanket on the bed or take to wearing pyjamas so that you can turn your heating off at night, even in the very cold weather.

☐ BICYCLE
Personal transportation choices can shrink your carbon footprint quite dramatically. Instead of taking your car out of the garage get on your bike. It will not only save you money, improve your health but it reduces pollution as well.

☐ BIODIESEL
If your car is suitable try running it on biodiesel or you could be really ambitious and adapt your car and make your own out of recycled cooking oil.

☐ BOILER
If your boiler is old consider replacing it with a high-efficiency condensing boiler. This type of appliance can help reduce heating-related carbon dioxide emissions by as much as 15–20 per cent.

☐ **BUY LOCAL PRODUCTS**

Practically everything we buy has its own carbon footprint whether it is transportation costs or the amount of electricity that goes into the manufacturing of the product or its packaging. Start by buying local produce, for example fruit and vegetables and local farm meat, wherever possible.

☐ **BUY PRODUCTS MADE OF RECYCLED PAPER**

If you want to know whether a package has been recycled, then you need to read the small print which should claim 'made of 100 per cent recycled material'. Some packages do not advertise this fact, but there are other ways of finding out. Check the colour of the card used to make cereal boxes. Just as an example, if the underside is grey or brown then this indicates that the cardboard is made of recycled materials. If it is white, however, it is made of virgin material.

☐ **CAR SHARING**

Try and organise a car-sharing scheme with your colleagues at work. It will make your travelling to and from work more economical and you are respecting the environment at the same time.

☐ **CARRIER BAGS**

Every time you go shopping take a reusable canvas bag with you so that you don't have to use the plastic carrier bags supplied by the supermarkets.

☐ **CHANGE A LIGHT BULB**

Replace your conventional light bulbs with energy-saving compact fluorescent bulbs. Start in places where lights are left on the longest. Although these bulbs cost more than conventional ones (about £6 each), not only do they use 75 per cent less electricity but they last eight times longer.

☐ CHOOSE A SHOWER

An average bath uses far more water than a five-minute shower, so change your bathing habits and keep it brief.

☐ CLOSE THE REFRIGERATOR DOOR

By leaving the refrigerator door open even for a few extra seconds, you are wasting a lot of energy. Decide what you want before opening the door, take it out and close the door right away. While on the subject of the refrigerator, make sure you keep it regularly defrosted and that the coils are dust free. Replace any damaged door seals as these will allow heat in and waste further energy trying to keep the inside cool.

☐ CODDLE YOUR TANK

Coddle your hot water tank by treating it to a nice thick insulating jacket. While you are doing this check the water temperature setting — it should be no higher than 60°C (140°F).

☐ COMPOST

Find a corner of your garden that is out of the way and start creating your own compost. As you gradually build up the pile using your garden and kitchen waste you will be turning your 'rubbish' into a valuable fertiliser for your soil.

☐ CURTAINS

Take advantage of natural sunlight to warm your rooms by making sure that your curtains are open as soon as you get up. At night, close them as soon as it gets dark to retain the heat.

☐ CUT DOWN ON PACKAGING

Try very hard not to buy produce that is packaged unnecessarily. Refuse to put your carrots into the plastic bags provided or to buy that sweetcorn that is sitting in a non-biodegradable polystyrene tray, and be aware that you are doing something to reduce that mountain of garbage building up at the landfill sites.

☐ DONATE YOUR TOYS

When your child outgrows its toys or simply gets tired of them, don't throw them away. Give them to a worthy cause; there is always some child somewhere in the world who will benefit. Even if they are broken, some charities can get them fixed and give them to a needy cause.

☐ DON'T BUY AEROSOLS

Because the majority of aerosols cannot be recycled, think twice before buying something that is packaged in that way. Aerosols will end up on landfill sites and contribute to air pollution. Look for spray bottles, liquids, powders and roll-ons as a substitute.

☐ DOUBLE GLAZING

It is well worth having double glazing fitted in your home; it is an outlay that will eventually save you a lot of money. Start with the rooms that cost the most to heat and choose windows that have the 'energy saving recommended' logo. A cheaper alternative would be to fit secondary glazing.

☐ DRAUGHTS

Carry a lit stick of incense slowly around your house and wherever the smoke blows horizontally means that you have a draught. The most likely sources will be fireplaces, windows, door frames, letterboxes and cat flaps. Next put draught excluder (available from your DIY store) on all the places where you are losing heat. It is probably better to leave kitchen and bathroom windows alone to minimise the risk of condensation.

☐ **DRIPPING TAP**

Fix that dripping tap because it can waste as much as a bathful of water each week.

☐ **EAT ORGANIC**

Organic produce contains far fewer chemicals than other produce. For this reason it is definitely better for the environment and most probably for your health as well. Remember that any chemicals used to treat produce get washed into the soil and eventually seep into our water supply.

☐ **EGG BOXES**

Avoid eggs that are packaged in polystyrene or other non-biodegradable materials. Only buy eggs that come in cartons made from paper pulp. These can be used as seed trays when you have finished with them as they are ideal for bringing on those precious seedlings.

☐ **ENDANGERED SPECIES**

Encourage people not to buy anything made from things like natural fur, ivory, corals or any other products that have come from endangered species. You can also avoid buying certain types of pets, for example exotic birds that have been taken away from their natural habitat.

☐ **ENERGY SUPPLIER**

It is worth checking to see whether you are using the cheapest energy supplier. You may be able to save money by switching or opt for a company that offers a green tariff. Companies such as Good Energy and Green Energy in the UK invest in building renewable energy projects so that they actively cut the amount of fossil fuels burned and do their part to reduce global warming.

☐ ENERGY WASTERS

Take note of any companies in your area that are unnecessarily wasting our precious resources. For example, a car showroom that leaves its lights shining all night, or someone picking up their child from school who sits with their car engine idling. Don't just turn a blind eye, say something or write a letter asking them not to waste energy.

☐ FARMERS' MARKETS

Support your local farmers and buy your produce from a farmers' market. A farmers' market is a venue for local farmers and people making food with local ingredients, who must live within a 30-mile radius.

☐ FEED THE BIRDS

Birds, like humans, need food and water. Feeding birds not only helps to bring a bit of nature into your garden, but it also helps destroy some of the unwanted insects but in a natural way. You can either hang a birdfeeder from a tree so that you can see it from your window, or put a bird table and birdbath in your garden.

☐ FLOORS

Fill those gaps between your old floorboards and skirting board with commercial sealant. Alternatively, you could try using papier mâché, both will help cut out the draughts.

☐ GLASS

Glass is one of the best materials for recycling as it can be recycled again and again, saving both energy and raw materials. Before recycling make sure you remove any lids and that the bottles or jars have been washed. Also make sure that you put them in the right coloured banks as any contamination will lower the value of the recycled glass.

☐ GREENER DRIVER

If you are thinking of changing your car, try and be aware of the environment and opt for a more fuel efficient car. If you are lucky enough to be able to afford a hybrid car you could save as much as 16,000 pounds of carbon dioxide emissions each year, a large chunk out of your carbon footprint.

☐ 'GREEN' PICNIC

If you are planning to have a picnic make sure you keep it 'green'. For example, if you are using a barbecue, avoid using lighter fluid (an air pollutant). Try using a match and some newspaper instead. Use real plates and cutlery and reusable cups instead of paper and plastic. In that way you can use everything over and over again. Remember, just because you are outdoors it doesn't mean you can make a lot of extra waste.

☐ GROW A GARDEN

A garden provides flowers, vegetables, trees and encourages other environmental benefits. It can help to reduce soil erosion and may help to reduce air pollution. Try to grow your garden using as few pesticides and chemical fertilisers as possible.

☐ HAZARDOUS WASTE

Nearly every household throws out some type of hazardous waste — for example old paint cans, used motor oil, unused pesticides and weedkillers. If you simply pour these substances down the drain you will end up polluting the water supply. They should be disposed of at a site that has been specially set up for hazardous or toxic waste. Call your local council to find out the proper way to dispose of your hazardous waste.

☐ HELIUM BALLOONS

Helium balloons are a lot of fun, especially when you let them float up into the sky. Did you know though that they could be harmful to fish and animals. Helium balloons will eventually fall back to Earth and can be blown for many miles out to sea. Some sea animals could mistake the baloon for something to eat and it could kill. Make sure your child holds on tightly to the balloon, or even better tie it to something safe. If you know that someone intends to use helium balloons at a forthcoming celebration, point out the dangers of letting them fly away.

☐ HOT WATER

If you normally add cold water to your washing-up water, try turning down the thermostat on your boiler to 60°C (140°F). This could save you quite a few pounds each year.

☐ INSULATE

You will probably find that you are wasting a lot of energy in your home without really realising. Take time to have an energy check and find out where you can save energy and money. Things like loft insulation, lagging hot water pipes and tanks and cavity wall insulation can all help reduce the energy output of your house. You may also be able to get energy saving grants to help you with the cost. Building regulations on new homes requires a minimum of 250 millimetres (10 inches) loft insulation. If doing this yourself make sure you leave gaps around the eaves to avoid causing condensation.

☐ JUNK MAIL
Act today to stop junk mail by putting a sticker on your letterbox or by contacting the Mail Preference Service to have your name taken off the register.

☐ KETTLE
Only boil as much water as you need each time you use the kettle to save on energy.

☐ LIDS
Make sure you use lids when you are cooking as it means that food will reach boiling point far quicker and take less time to cook.

☐ LINE CURTAINS
Put a lining in your curtains to help with insulation and minimise the loss of heat through your windows.

☐ LOOK AT LABELS
Reading labels can tell you a lot about a product you are about to buy. If you are unsure or unhappy about any of the ingredients and feel they could be hazardous to your health or environment, make the manufacturer aware. They will be only too pleased to listen to what you have to say and it doesn't take too many letters before a manufacturer will consider making changes.

☐ MAKE NOTEPADS

Instead of throwing away all that paper, recycle it by making notepads which you can use for a shopping list or for scoring in that game of cards. Put the blank sides face up and staple a batch together.

☐ OBSERVE THE THREE 'Rs'

REFUSE . . . REUSE . . . RECYCLE. These are the three most important rules to live by as far as the environment is concerned. Next time you go shopping, whether you are on your own, with your children or friends, get everyone to think about the three Rs every time you take something off the shelf. Is it something that you really need, is it over-packaged or is it something you can reuse? If the answer is NO to these questions then refuse.

☐ PICK IT UP

Next time you are out for a walk or a picnic and you see litter lying around, why not pick it up and throw it in the nearest bin. If everyone does the same thing our planet would be a far cleaner place.

☐ PLANT A TREE

Wouldn't it be nice to plant your own tree and watch it grow over the years? There are organisations in most communities today that have set up tree-planting campaigns, and your local nursery is probably the best place to start. You can have the pleasure of watching it grow year by year and also know that other people will get pleasure out of it as well.

☐ PLASTIC

Most types of plastic are suitable for recycling, but some types of plastic are much easier than others. A general rule is that local authorities that recycle plastic will only accept items with a '1' or '2' in a triangle on the bottom of the container, so it is worth checking before buying anything in a plastic container.

☐ **PROTEST**

Make your views known about animal cruelty. Every year certain industries still use laboratory animals — rats, mice, dogs, monkeys and others — which all suffer needlessly because companies want to test some new cosmetic, for example. These animals are routinely burned, injected with poisonous substances and suffer other horrendous experiments. Make sure you protest by choosing a product that is labelled CRUELTY FREE and if everyone does the same thing the manufacturers will soon get the hint.

☐ **QUIT**

Stop throwing away batteries, because they contain hazardous materials that leak into landfill sites and subsequently end up in our water supply. There are two ways to stop — use rechargeable batteries or find out if there is a company in your area that recycles used batteries. Another idea is to send the batteries back to the manufacturers, saying that you consider them to be hazardous waste. Lastly, ask yourself whether you need to use so many products that require a battery.

☐ **RADIATORS**

Slide aluminium foil behind any radiators that are fitted to an outside wall to help keep heat in the room. Ordinary household foil will do, or you can buy specially designed panels. Consider fitting thermostatic valves (around £6 each) to each radiator so that you can control the amount of heat emitted by each appliance. Ask yourself whether you really need a radiator on in a room that is not being used on a regular basis. Finally, although it might sound odd, putting a shelf above a radiator actually deflects heat back into the room. Also avoid putting furniture in front of a radiator as this will only waste heat as it can't penetrate the whole room.

☐ RECYCLE

Make sure you recycle everything easibly possible. Set up recycling boxes in your home and if you can't recycle something try and find another way of using it.

☐ RECYCLED PAPER

Buy recycled paper whenever it is available. In most cases you can buy toilet paper, paper towels, napkins, writing books, books, newspapers and many other things made out of recycled paper.

☐ SOLAR PANELS

With constantly increasing prices from our energy suppliers consider installing a solar panel. On a sunny day you can get enough energy to run a 100W light from just one square metre of solar panel. Alternatively, you could use it to supply your hot water.

☐ STANDBY MODE

Make sure you don't leave electrical appliances on standby mode. TVs, videos, computers and stereos when left in standby mode can use as much as 70 per cent of the energy they use when they are switched on.

☐ SWITCH IT OFF

Make sure you turn off lights in rooms that you are not occupying. If your children are bad at leaving lights on then think about putting bright labels near the light switch to remind them to turn them off.

☐ **TAKE A WALK**

The next time you are going down the road to the local shops why not stop and think about walking instead of taking the car. In your free time encourage your children to walk and get them to appreciate the beauty of the countryside around them. Also walk your children to school instead of driving, because a fifth of the cars on our roads in the morning peak period are parents driving their children to school.

☐ **TALK**

Talk to your children and make them aware of green issues so that they can learn ways to make the world a better place for future generations. Hopefully, with the help of education, our children will know more about the environment than we do.

☐ **TOILET**

You can safely reduce the amount of water released by each flush of your toilet. A produce like Ecoflush regulates the amount of water used, costs around £20 and you can install it yourself. Alternatively, a toilet hippo will cut the volume of water flushed by one-third and is especially useful in toilets installed before 1993 as they have larger cisterns. Some water companies supply hippos for free.

☐ **TUMBLE DRYER**

Give your tumble dryer a rest in the summer and hang your washing out to dry. The sun can help bleach out stains too and keep your whites white.

☐ **TURN IT DOWN**

Turn your central heating thermostat down by one degree and save up to £30 a year on your heating bill.

☐ USE BOTH SIDES

Use both sides of paper at work and home and encourage your colleagues to do the same. Also think very carefully before you print anything out, is it really necessary?

☐ WIND TURBINES

The use of wind turbines can be a great way to provide a source of clean and renewable energy for your home or business. There are a number of small wind energy devices that you can use to generate power, and most of these are very cost-effective in providing a substantial level of electricity. You will, of course, need to get permission from the council before you can embark on this project.

☐ WRITE A SHOPPING LIST

By writing a shopping list you can make sure you don't come home with far more than you need.

Go on, start your 'Green Diet' today and see just how easy it is to change the way you look at things. You will be amazed at just how much you can save in the way of money and the cost to the environment.
